SEO-Friendly Website Building: A Beginner's Guide

Chapter 1: Introduction to SEO
1.1 Understanding Search Engine Optimization
Understanding Search Engine Optimization (SEO) is crucial for anyone looking to improve the visibility and organic ranking of their website on search engine results pages (SERPs). SEO refers to the practices and techniques used to optimize websites and make them more relevant and appealing to search engines.

At its core, SEO aims to enhance the website's visibility to attract more organic traffic from search engines like Google, Bing, and Yahoo. By understanding how search engines work and what factors influence their rankings, website owners and marketers can strategically optimize their websites to achieve higher rankings and increase their chances of being found by their target audience.

Key aspects of understanding SEO include:

1. Keyword Research: SEO begins with identifying relevant keywords and phrases that people are using to search for information related to your website's content or industry. Keyword research helps determine the terms you should target in your optimization efforts.

2. On-Page Optimization: This involves optimizing various elements on your web pages, including titles, meta descriptions, headings, and content, to make them more relevant to search queries and improve the overall user experience.

3. Off-Page Optimization: Off-page optimization focuses on building backlinks from reputable and relevant websites to improve your website's authority and credibility. It also involves social media promotion, guest blogging, and other strategies to increase the visibility and reach of your website.

4. Technical SEO: Technical SEO ensures that your website is properly structured and optimized for search engines to crawl and index its pages effectively. It involves optimizing site speed, improving mobile responsiveness, using XML sitemaps, and implementing schema markup.

5. Content Creation: Creating high-quality, informative, and engaging content is an essential part of SEO. Publishing valuable content helps attract organic traffic, encourages backlinks, and establishes your website as a trustworthy source of information.

6. User Experience: User experience plays a significant role in SEO. Websites that provide a seamless, intuitive, and enjoyable user experience tend to rank higher. Factors like site speed, mobile-friendliness, easy navigation, and responsive design contribute to a positive user experience.

7. Analytics and Monitoring: Analysing website traffic, user behavior, and conversion rates using tools like Google Analytics helps you understand the effectiveness of your SEO efforts. Monitoring and tracking data allow you to make data-driven decisions and refine your strategies over time.

By gaining a thorough understanding of SEO, you can optimize your website to attract organic traffic, increase visibility, and achieve higher rankings in search engine results. It is an ongoing process that requires continuous monitoring, adjustments, and adaptation to keep up with search engine algorithms and user expectations.

1.2 Importance of an SEO-Friendly Website
An SEO-friendly website is of paramount importance in today's digital landscape. Here are some key reasons highlighting the significance of having an SEO-friendly website:

1. Increased Organic Visibility: An SEO-friendly website is more likely to appear in the top positions of search engine results pages (SERPs). This visibility translates into higher organic traffic, as users tend to click on the top-ranking results.

2. Targeted Traffic: SEO helps optimize your website for specific keywords and phrases relevant to your business. This means that when users search for those keywords, your website has a better chance of appearing in front of a targeted audience actively seeking information or solutions related to your industry.

3. Enhanced User Experience: SEO involves optimizing various elements of your website, such as page load speed, mobile responsiveness, easy navigation, and informative content. These optimizations result in an improved user experience, leading to longer website visits, reduced bounce rates, and increased engagement.

4. Competitive Advantage: In today's highly competitive digital landscape, having an SEO-friendly website gives you an edge over competitors who may not be investing in SEO. By outranking competitors in search engine results, you can attract more organic traffic and capture a larger share of the market.

5. Long-Term Cost Savings: While implementing SEO strategies may require an initial investment, the long-term benefits can outweigh the costs. Unlike paid advertising, which stops generating traffic once you stop paying, SEO efforts can continue driving organic traffic to your website over an extended period.

6. Brand Credibility and Trust: Appearing in top search engine results positions establishes your brand as a credible and trustworthy source. Users often associate higher search rankings with reliability, which can enhance your brand's reputation and increase user trust.

7. Measurable Results: SEO allows you to track and measure the impact of your efforts using analytics tools. You can monitor website traffic, keyword rankings, conversion rates, and other metrics to gain insights into the effectiveness of your SEO strategies and make data-driven decisions.

8. Adaptability to Algorithm Changes: Search engine algorithms evolve continuously, and an SEO-friendly website is better equipped to adapt to these changes. By following SEO best practices and staying updated with algorithm updates, you can maintain and improve your website's ranking and visibility.

In summary, having an SEO-friendly website is crucial for attracting targeted organic traffic, enhancing user experience, establishing brand credibility, and gaining a competitive advantage in the digital landscape. By investing in SEO, you can drive long-term growth and success for your online presence.

1.3 Key SEO Concepts and Terminologies
To effectively navigate the world of SEO, it is essential to understand key concepts and terminologies. Here are some fundamental SEO concepts you should be familiar with:

1. Keywords: These are the words or phrases users enter into search engines when looking for information. Keywords play a vital role in SEO as they help determine the relevance of your content to user queries.

2. On-Page Optimization: This refers to optimizing various elements on your web pages to improve their visibility and relevance to search engines. It includes optimizing titles, meta descriptions, headings, URLs, and content for targeted keywords.

3. Off-Page Optimization: Off-page optimization focuses on activities conducted outside your website to improve its visibility and reputation. It primarily involves building high-quality backlinks from other authoritative websites, as well as social media promotion and online mentions.

4. Organic Traffic: Organic traffic refers to visitors who find your website through unpaid search engine results. It is considered highly valuable as it signifies users actively seeking relevant information or solutions.

5. SERPs: Short for Search Engine Results Pages, SERPs are the pages displayed by search engines in response to a user's query. These pages list websites ranked according to their relevance and authority.

6. Crawling and Indexing: Search engines use crawlers (also known as spiders or bots) to explore and analyze websites. Crawling involves the process of discovering web pages, while indexing refers to storing and organizing the information found during crawling.

7. Backlinks: These are links from external websites that point to your website. Backlinks are crucial for SEO as they serve as a vote of confidence and can improve your website's authority and rankings.

8. PageRank: PageRank is an algorithm developed by Google to determine the importance and relevance of web pages. It evaluates the quality and quantity of backlinks to a page to assess its authority.

9. Meta Tags: These are HTML tags that provide information about a web page's content to search engines. The two most common meta tags are the title tag, which specifies the page title displayed in search results, and the meta description tag, which provides a brief summary of the page.

10. Canonicalization: Canonicalization is the process of selecting the preferred URL format for a webpage when multiple URLs with similar content exist. It helps search engines understand which URL should be indexed and displayed in search results.

11. Algorithm Updates: Search engines regularly update their algorithms to provide more accurate and relevant search results. These updates can impact website rankings, and staying informed about them is crucial for maintaining SEO success.

By familiarizing yourself with these key SEO concepts and terminologies, you'll be better equipped to optimize your website, understand industry discussions, and make informed decisions to improve your online visibility and rankings

Chapter-2
Keyword Research and Analysis

2.1 Importance of Keyword Research

Keyword research is of utmost importance in SEO as it lays the foundation for your website's visibility and relevance in search engine results. Here are some key reasons why keyword research is essential:

1. Understanding User Intent: Keyword research helps you gain insights into the language, phrases, and queries users use when searching for information related to your industry or business. By understanding user intent, you can align your website's content with what users are actively seeking.

2. Targeting Relevant Traffic: Effective keyword research enables you to identify high-potential keywords that are relevant to your products, services, or content. By targeting these keywords in your optimization efforts, you can attract highly targeted and relevant traffic to your website.

3. Competition Analysis: Keyword research allows you to analyze the keywords your competitors are targeting and ranking for. This information helps you identify opportunities, find gaps in the market, and develop a strategy to outrank your competition.

4. Content Creation and Optimization: Keyword research provides valuable insights into the topics and themes that resonate with your target audience. By incorporating relevant keywords into your content, you can optimize it for search engines, improve its visibility, and increase its chances of ranking higher in search results.

5. Long-Tail Keywords: Keyword research helps uncover long-tail keywords, which are longer and more specific keyword phrases. While they may have lower search volumes, they often indicate a higher level of user intent and can drive targeted traffic to your website. Long-tail keywords also have less competition, making it easier to rank for them.

6. Website Architecture and Structure: Keyword research plays a crucial role in structuring your website and organizing your content. By mapping keywords to specific pages or sections of your website, you can create a clear and user-friendly navigation structure that aligns with user search behaviour.

7. Pay-Per-Click (PPC) Advertising: Keyword research is vital in PPC advertising campaigns, where targeting the right keywords can maximize the effectiveness of your ad campaigns and optimize your budget allocation.

8. Topic Expansion and Content Strategy: Keyword research helps identify related topics and subtopics that you can incorporate into your content strategy. It allows you to expand your content offerings and provide comprehensive information that covers various aspects of your industry or niche.

By investing time and effort in keyword research, you can ensure that your website is optimized for the right keywords, attracts relevant traffic, and improves its visibility and rankings in search engine results. It forms the backbone of your SEO strategy and is a critical step in driving organic traffic and achieving online success.

2.2 Tools and Techniques for Keyword Research
When it comes to keyword research, there are various tools and techniques available to help you discover valuable keywords for your SEO efforts. Here are some popular tools and techniques:

1. Google Keyword Planner: This free tool from Google Ads provides keyword ideas, search volume data, and competition levels. It is an excellent starting point for keyword research and offers insights into the popularity of specific keywords.

2. Google Trends: Google Trends helps you identify trending topics and keywords by showing their search volume over time. It can be helpful in understanding seasonal trends and the popularity of specific search terms.

3. SEMrush: SEMrush is a comprehensive SEO tool that offers robust keyword research capabilities. It provides keyword suggestions, search volume data, keyword difficulty scores, and competitive analysis. SEMrush also offers insights into your competitors' top-ranking keywords.

4. Ahrefs: Ahrefs is another powerful SEO tool that offers extensive keyword research features. It provides keyword suggestions, search volume data, keyword difficulty scores, and backlink analysis. Ahrefs also offers valuable insights into competitors' keywords and content gaps.

5. Moz Keyword Explorer: Moz's Keyword Explorer provides keyword suggestions, search volume data, and difficulty scores. It also offers insights into related keywords and provides recommendations for optimizing your content.

6. Long-Tail Pro: Long-Tail Pro is a popular keyword research tool specifically focused on discovering long-tail keywords. It helps identify low-competition keywords that can drive targeted traffic to your website.

7. Keyword Research Techniques: In addition to using keyword research tools, you can employ various techniques such as analysing competitor websites, exploring related searches on search engines, utilizing question-and-answer platforms like Quora, and conducting customer surveys to gather insights into the language and terms used by your target audience.

When performing keyword research, it is essential to consider factors like search volume, keyword difficulty, relevance to your target audience, and the competitiveness of your industry. Combining multiple keyword research tools and techniques will give you a comprehensive understanding of valuable keywords to target in your SEO strategy.

Remember to choose keywords that align with your website's content, user intent, and business goals. Prioritize long-tail keywords, as they often have higher conversion rates and lower competition. Regularly monitor and update your keyword strategy to stay ahead of evolving search trends and user behaviour.

2.3 Analysing Keyword Competition and Search Volume
Analysing keyword competition and search volume is essential for effective keyword research. It helps you understand the level of competition you'll face and the potential traffic you can expect from targeting specific keywords. Here are some techniques to analyze keyword competition and search volume:

1. Search Volume Analysis:
   - Use keyword research tools like Google Keyword Planner, SEMrush, or Ahrefs to get search volume data for your target keywords. These tools provide an estimate of how many times a keyword is searched for in a given period.
   - Compare the search volume of different keywords to identify high-volume keywords that are relevant to your content or business. Focus on keywords that have a substantial search volume to ensure a meaningful impact on your website's traffic.
   - Look for seasonal trends in search volume to understand when certain keywords are more popular. This can help you align your content and marketing efforts accordingly.

2. Competition Analysis:
   - Use keyword research tools to assess keyword competition. These tools provide insights into the level of competition for a specific keyword, often represented by a difficulty score or a competitive index.
   - Analyze the top-ranking pages for your target keywords on search engine results pages (SERPs). Evaluate factors like domain authority, page authority, backlink profile, and content quality to understand the strength of your competitors.
   - Pay attention to the number and quality of backlinks pointing to competitor pages targeting the same keywords. This can give you an idea of the effort required to outrank them.

3. Long-Tail Keywords:
   - Long-tail keywords are longer and more specific search queries that usually have lower search volume but lower competition as well. Analyze long-tail keywords relevant to your content or business to find opportunities with a higher chance of ranking.
   - Long-tail keywords often indicate higher user intent and can attract more targeted traffic to your website. They are particularly useful for niche businesses or websites with specific content offerings.

4. Keyword Difficulty:
   - Some keyword research tools provide a keyword difficulty metric that indicates the level of competition for a keyword. This metric takes into account various factors, such as backlink profiles and domain authority of the top-ranking pages.
   - Focus on keywords with a moderate difficulty level that strike a balance between search volume and competition. Targeting keywords with extremely high competition may require significant resources and time to rank effectively.

By analysing keyword competition and search volume, you can identify valuable keywords with a balance of high search volume and manageable competition. This helps you prioritize your keyword targeting, optimize your content, and improve your chances of ranking higher in search engine results. Regularly monitor and update your keyword strategy to adapt to changes in search trends and stay ahead of your competitors. Analysing keyword competition and search volume is essential for effective keyword research. It helps you understand the level of competition you'll face and the potential traffic you can expect from targeting specific keywords. Here are some techniques to analyze keyword competition and search volume:

1. Search Volume Analysis:
   - Use keyword research tools like Google Keyword Planner, SEMrush, or Ahrefs to get search volume data for your target keywords. These tools provide an estimate of how many times a keyword is searched for in a given period.

- Compare the search volume of different keywords to identify high-volume keywords that are relevant to your content or business. Focus on keywords that have a substantial search volume to ensure a meaningful impact on your website's traffic.
   - Look for seasonal trends in search volume to understand when certain keywords are more popular. This can help you align your content and marketing efforts accordingly.

2. Competition Analysis:
   - Use keyword research tools to assess keyword competition. These tools provide insights into the level of competition for a specific keyword, often represented by a difficulty score or a competitive index.
   - Analyze the top-ranking pages for your target keywords on search engine results pages (SERPs). Evaluate factors like domain authority, page authority, backlink profile, and content quality to understand the strength of your competitors.
   - Pay attention to the number and quality of backlinks pointing to competitor pages targeting the same keywords. This can give you an idea of the effort required to outrank them.

3. Long-Tail Keywords:
   - Long-tail keywords are longer and more specific search queries that usually have lower search volume but lower competition as well. Analyze long-tail keywords relevant to your content or business to find opportunities with a higher chance of ranking.
   - Long-tail keywords often indicate higher user intent and can attract more targeted traffic to your website. They are particularly useful for niche businesses or websites with specific content offerings.

4. Keyword Difficulty:
   - Some keyword research tools provide a keyword difficulty metric that indicates the level of competition for a keyword. This metric takes into account various factors, such as backlink profiles and domain authority of the top-ranking pages.
   - Focus on keywords with a moderate difficulty level that strike a balance between search volume and competition. Targeting keywords with extremely high competition may require significant resources and time to rank effectively.

By analysing keyword competition and search volume, you can identify valuable keywords with a balance of high search volume and manageable competition. This helps you prioritize your keyword targeting, optimize your content, and improve your chances of ranking higher in search engine results. Regularly monitor and update your keyword strategy to adapt to changes in search trends and stay ahead of your competitors.

2.4 Long-Tail Keywords and their Significance
Long-tail keywords are longer and more specific search queries that typically have lower search volume but higher conversion rates. Here's why long-tail keywords are significant in SEO:

1. Targeted and Relevant Traffic: Long-tail keywords provide a more precise understanding of user intent. By targeting specific phrases or questions, you can attract highly targeted traffic that is more likely to convert. Long-tail keywords often reflect users who are further along in their buying journey and have a specific need or problem they are looking to solve.

2. Lower Competition: Long-tail keywords usually have lower competition compared to generic or highly competitive keywords. This means it's easier to rank for long-tail keywords, especially if you have a niche or specialized business. Focusing on long-tail keywords allows you to capture a specific audience without having to compete with larger, more established websites.

3. Higher Conversion Rates: Users searching with long-tail keywords are typically looking for specific information, products, or services. Because long-tail keywords align closely with their search intent, visitors who arrive at your website through long-tail keyword searches are more likely to convert into leads or customers. Long-tail keywords often lead to higher conversion rates compared to broader, more generic keywords.

4. Improved Content Relevance: Long-tail keywords provide opportunities to create highly targeted and relevant content. By addressing specific queries or topics related to long-tail keywords, you can deliver valuable and comprehensive information that satisfies user intent. This can enhance the user experience and establish your website as a reliable source of information in your niche.

5. Voice Search Optimization: With the rise of voice assistants and smart devices, the use of long-tail keywords has become even more important. Voice searches are often conversational and include longer, more specific queries. Optimizing your content for long-tail keywords improves your chances of appearing in voice search results.

6. Niche Marketing Opportunities: Long-tail keywords are particularly valuable for businesses operating in niche markets or offering specialized products or services. By targeting long-tail keywords specific to your niche, you can attract a highly relevant audience interested in your unique offerings.

To leverage the significance of long-tail keywords:
- Conduct thorough keyword research to identify relevant long-tail keywords related to your business.
- Create content that directly addresses user queries or problems associated with long-tail keywords.
- Optimize your web pages with long-tail keywords in titles, headings, meta descriptions, and content.
- Monitor and analyze the performance of your long-tail keyword-focused content to refine and improve your strategy over time.

By incorporating long-tail keywords into your SEO strategy, you can attract highly targeted traffic, improve conversion rates, and establish your website as a valuable resource in your niche.

Chapter-3
On-Page Optimization

3.1 Optimizing Page Titles and Meta Descriptions

Optimizing page titles and meta descriptions is crucial for improving your website's visibility in search engine results and attracting click-throughs from users. Here's how you can optimize these elements:

1. Page Titles:
- Keep it concise: Ensure that your page titles are clear, concise, and accurately represent the content of the page. Aim for a length of around 50-60 characters to avoid truncation in search engine results.
- Include target keywords: Incorporate relevant keywords naturally within the page title to indicate the topic and relevance of the content. However, prioritize readability and user experience over keyword stuffing.
- Unique titles: Each page should have a unique page title that accurately reflects the specific content and purpose of that page. Avoid using duplicate page titles, as it can confuse search engines and users.
- Branding: Consider including your brand name in the page title, especially for important or high-level pages. This can help with brand recognition and differentiate your content from competitors.

2. Meta Descriptions:
- Be compelling and informative: Write compelling meta descriptions that entice users to click through to your page. Clearly communicate what the page offers and why users should visit it. Keep the length within 150-160 characters to avoid truncation.
- Incorporate keywords: While meta descriptions don't directly impact search engine rankings, including relevant keywords can help improve visibility and relevance in search results.
- Unique descriptions: Just like page titles, each page should have a unique meta description that accurately describes its content. Avoid using duplicate meta descriptions, as it can negatively affect user experience and search engine rankings.
- Call-to-action (CTA): Consider adding a compelling CTA within the meta description to encourage users to click through to your page. For example, phrases like "Learn more," "Discover," or "Find out how" can be effective in driving clicks.

3. User-focused language: Write page titles and meta descriptions with your target audience in mind. Use language that resonates with them, addresses their needs, and clearly communicates the benefits or value they can expect from your page.

4. Review and update: Regularly review your page titles and meta descriptions to ensure they align with your current content and reflect any updates or changes. Monitor their performance in search results and make adjustments as needed to improve click-through rates.

Remember, optimizing page titles and meta descriptions is an ongoing process. Continuously analyze their performance, experiment with different approaches, and adapt to changes in search engine algorithms and user behaviour. By crafting compelling and informative page titles and meta descriptions, you can improve your website's click-through rates and attract more relevant traffic from search engine results.

3.2 Creating SEO-Friendly URLs
Creating SEO-friendly URLs is essential for search engine optimization and improving the visibility of your web pages. Here are some tips for creating SEO-friendly URLs:

1. Keep it concise and descriptive: Opt for short and descriptive URLs that accurately represent the content of the page. Use relevant keywords that give users and search engines an idea of what to expect when they click on the URL. Avoid long and convoluted URLs that are difficult to read and understand.

2. Use hyphens to separate words: Instead of using spaces or underscores, use hyphens (-) to separate words in your URLs. Hyphens make the URL more readable for both users and search engines. For example, use "my-website.com/seo-friendly-urls" instead of "my-website.com/seo_friendly_urls" or "my-website.com/seofriendlyurls".

3. Exclude unnecessary characters and symbols: Remove any unnecessary characters, symbols, or special characters from your URLs. Stick to alphanumeric characters and hyphens. Avoid using special characters, such as question marks, ampersands, or hash symbols, as they can cause issues with URL parsing and indexing.

4. Prioritize keywords: Include relevant keywords in your URLs, preferably towards the beginning. This helps search engines understand the topic of your page and can improve your chances of ranking for those keywords. However, avoid keyword stuffing or creating overly long URLs that become spammy or difficult to read.

5. Avoid dynamic parameters: If possible, avoid using dynamic parameters or query strings in your URLs. These are often associated with dynamically generated or session-specific content. Instead, aim for static and clean URLs that are more user-friendly and easier to index.

6. Canonicalize duplicate content URLs: If you have multiple URLs that point to the same content, use canonical tags to indicate the preferred URL. Canonical tags help search engines understand which version of the URL should be indexed and displayed in search results, reducing the risk of duplicate content issues.

7. Use lowercase letters: To maintain consistency and avoid confusion, use lowercase letters in your URLs. Differentiating between uppercase and lowercase versions of the same URL can lead to duplicate content issues and impact your SEO efforts.

8. Consider folder structure: Organize your URLs into logical folder structures that reflect the hierarchy of your website. This can make your URLs more intuitive and user-friendly. For example, use "my-website.com/blog/post-title" instead of "my-website.com/post-title" for blog posts.

By following these best practices, you can create SEO-friendly URLs that improve the visibility and accessibility of your web pages. Remember to consider both search engine optimization and user experience when crafting your URLs, as user-friendly URLs are more likely to be clicked and shared.

3.3 Header Tags and Heading Structure
Header tags and heading structure play a crucial role in organizing and presenting your content to both users and search engines. Here are some tips for using header tags effectively for SEO:

1. Use hierarchical structure: Structure your content with a logical hierarchy using header tags (H1, H2, H3, etc.). The H1 tag should be reserved for the main title of the page, while H2, H3, and

subsequent tags should be used for subheadings and subsections. This hierarchy helps search engines understand the organization of your content.

2. Include relevant keywords: Incorporate relevant keywords naturally within your header tags, especially in the H1 tag. This helps search engines determine the topic and relevance of your content. However, avoid keyword stuffing and focus on creating informative and engaging headings for users.

3. Maintain consistency: Use header tags consistently throughout your content. Avoid skipping heading levels or using header tags solely for styling purposes. Consistency in header tags helps both users and search engines understand the structure and flow of your content.

4. Make headings descriptive: Ensure that each heading accurately describes the content that follows it. Use clear and concise headings that provide a preview of the section's topic. Descriptive headings improve readability and help users navigate your content.

5. Use CSS for styling: Use Cascading Style Sheets (CSS) to style your headings rather than relying on header tags for formatting purposes. This ensures that your content remains accessible and allows search engines to focus on the semantic structure of your headings.

6. Avoid overusing H1 tags: Limit the use of H1 tags to a single instance per page. The H1 tag carries significant weight in signaling the main topic of the page, so using multiple H1 tags can confuse search engines and dilute the focus of your content.

7. Consider readability and visual hierarchy: In addition to SEO considerations, prioritize the readability and visual hierarchy of your headings. Use larger font sizes, appropriate font styles, and whitespace to enhance the readability and visual appeal of your headings.

8. Incorporate rich snippets: For certain types of content, consider implementing structured data markup to enhance your headings in search engine results. This can enable rich snippets like breadcrumbs or ratings, making your listings more appealing to users.

By following these best practices, you can optimize your header tags and heading structure for both search engines and users. Well-structured and descriptive headings improve the readability, organization, and overall SEO performance of your content.

3.4 Keyword Placement and Density
Keyword placement and density are important factors to consider when optimizing your content for search engines. Here are some tips for effectively placing keywords within your content:

1. Use keywords in the page title: Include your target keyword or a variation of it in the page title, preferably towards the beginning. This helps search engines understand the topic of your page and can improve your chances of ranking for that keyword.

2. Incorporate keywords in headings and subheadings: Use keywords naturally in your headings (H1, H2, etc.) and subheadings to signal the content's relevance to both search engines and users. This helps with the overall organization and structure of your content.

3. Include keywords in the URL: Incorporate your target keyword in the URL of the page, preferably towards the beginning. A keyword-rich URL helps search engines and users quickly identify the topic of the page.

4. Integrate keywords in the content body: Place keywords strategically throughout the content, ensuring they flow naturally and fit within the context. Avoid overusing keywords, as this can negatively impact readability and keyword stuffing can lead to penalties from search engines.

5. Use keywords in image alt text: Optimize your images by including relevant keywords in the alt text. This helps search engines understand the content of the image and can improve its visibility in image search results.

6. Utilize keywords in meta descriptions: Include keywords in the meta description of your page, as this is often displayed in search engine results. While meta descriptions don't directly impact rankings, incorporating keywords can improve relevance and attract user clicks.

7. Consider keyword variations and synonyms: Incorporate variations and synonyms of your target keywords to make your content more comprehensive and natural-sounding. This helps capture a broader range of search queries and improves the overall user experience.

When it comes to keyword density, there is no specific formula or ideal percentage to follow. Focus on using keywords naturally and in a way that makes sense to readers. Keyword stuffing, where keywords are excessively repeated without context, should be avoided as it can lead to penalties from search engines.

Instead of obsessing over keyword density, prioritize creating high-quality, informative, and engaging content that provides value to your audience. Write for readers first, and optimize for search engines second. When your content is well-written and relevant, the keywords will naturally be incorporated in a way that benefits both users and search engine visibility.

Regularly analyze and monitor your content's performance using SEO tools and adjust your keyword placement as needed to improve rankings and user engagement.

3.5 Optimizing Images for SEO
Optimizing images for SEO is crucial for improving your website's visibility in image search results and enhancing overall website performance. Here are some tips to optimize your images for SEO:

1. Choose the right file format: Use appropriate image file formats such as JPEG, PNG, or WebP based on the type of image and its requirements. JPEG is suitable for photographs, while PNG is ideal for images with transparent backgrounds. WebP is a newer format that offers smaller file sizes without compromising quality, making it great for web optimization.

2. Compress image file sizes: Optimize your images by compressing them without sacrificing quality. Large image files can significantly impact page loading speed, leading to a poor user experience and lower search engine rankings. Use compression tools or plugins to reduce the file size of your images before uploading them to your website.

3. Resize images for web: Ensure that your images are appropriately sized for the web. Avoid uploading high-resolution images that are larger than what is necessary for display on your website. Use image editing software or online tools to resize your images to the dimensions needed for your web pages.

4. Use descriptive filenames: Give your image files descriptive and keyword-rich filenames. Avoid generic names like "image001.jpg" and instead use relevant keywords that accurately describe the image content. For example, use "seo-friendly-website.png" instead of "IMG1234.png". This helps search engines understand the context and relevance of the image.

5. Optimize alt text: Add descriptive and keyword-rich alt text (alternative text) to your images. Alt text provides a textual description of the image and is useful for users who cannot view images or for search engines to understand the content of the image. Use concise, meaningful, and accurate alt text that reflects the image and its relevance to the surrounding content.

6. Utilize image captions: If appropriate, include image captions that provide additional context and relevant information about the image. Captions can enhance the user experience and help search engines understand the image content better.

7. Implement structured data for images: Consider implementing structured data markup, such as schema.org, to provide additional information about your images to search engines. This can help search engines understand the subject matter of the image and potentially display rich snippets in search results.

8. Use responsive design: Ensure that your website is responsive and mobile-friendly, allowing images to scale appropriately for different devices and screen sizes. This improves user experience and SEO performance, as mobile-friendliness is a ranking factor for search engines.

By optimizing your images for SEO, you can improve your website's visibility in image search results, enhance user experience, and potentially attract more organic traffic. Regularly analyze your website's image performance and make adjustments as needed to ensure your images are optimized for both search engines and users.

3.6 Internal Linking Strategies
Internal linking is an important SEO strategy that involves linking pages within your own website. It helps search engines understand the structure and hierarchy of your website, establishes relationships between pages, and distributes link authority throughout your site. Here are some internal linking strategies to optimize your website:

1. Create a logical site structure: Organize your website into a logical hierarchy with clear categories and subcategories. This allows you to establish a clear pathway for users and search engines to navigate your site. Link from higher-level pages to more specific pages within the same category or topic.

2. Use descriptive anchor text: When creating internal links, use descriptive anchor text that accurately reflects the content of the target page. Avoid using generic anchor text like "click here" or "read more." Instead, use relevant keywords or phrases that provide context about the linked page.

3. Link from high-authority pages: Identify your high-authority pages, such as those with a significant number of inbound links or strong search engine rankings. From these pages, include internal links to other important pages on your website to pass on link authority and boost their visibility.

4. Prioritize user experience: Internal links should serve the user's needs by providing additional relevant information or guiding them to related content. Ensure that the linked pages are valuable

and enhance the user experience. Avoid excessive internal linking that may confuse or overwhelm users.

5. Use contextual linking: Incorporate internal links within the body of your content, where they are contextually relevant. For example, when discussing a topic, link to other related articles or resources that provide more in-depth information or support your points. This helps search engines understand the relationship between different pages.

6. Create hub pages: Hub pages act as centralized resources for specific topics or themes and link out to related pages or articles within your website. These hub pages help consolidate information and improve the internal linking structure of your site.

7. Update and maintain your internal links: Regularly review and update your internal links to ensure they remain accurate and relevant. Broken or outdated internal links can negatively impact user experience and SEO. Use tools to periodically check for broken links and fix them promptly.

8. Utilize sitemaps: Include a sitemap on your website that lists all the pages you want to be indexed by search engines. This helps search engines discover and crawl your pages more efficiently. Additionally, ensure your sitemap includes updated internal links as you add or modify pages on your site.

Remember that while internal linking is important for SEO, it should be done in a natural and user-friendly manner. Focus on providing value to your users and creating a cohesive and organized website structure. By implementing effective internal linking strategies, you can improve user navigation, enhance search engine visibility, and increase the overall SEO performance of your website.

Chapter 4:
Technical SEO

4.1 Website Speed and Performance Optimization
Website speed and performance optimization is crucial for providing a positive user experience, reducing bounce rates, and improving search engine rankings. Here are some strategies to optimize the speed and performance of your website:

1. Optimize images: Compress and resize images to reduce their file size without compromising quality. Use image formats like JPEG or WebP, enable lazy loading to load images only when they come into view, and leverage caching techniques to store images locally for faster loading.

2. Minify CSS, JavaScript, and HTML: Minify your code by removing unnecessary spaces, comments, and line breaks. This reduces file sizes and improves load times. Additionally, combine multiple CSS and JavaScript files into single files to minimize the number of requests made to the server.

3. Enable browser caching: Set up caching headers to enable browser caching. This allows returning visitors to load your website faster by storing static files in their browser cache. Configure caching to specify how long different file types should be cached to strike a balance between fresh content and performance.

4. Use a content delivery network (CDN): Implement a CDN to distribute your website's static files across multiple servers worldwide. This reduces the distance between the user and the server, resulting in faster loading times. The CDN automatically serves files from the nearest server location.

5. Optimize code and scripts: Review and optimize your website's code and scripts to remove any unnecessary or inefficient code. Eliminate render-blocking JavaScript and CSS, and place JavaScript files at the bottom of the page to prevent them from blocking page rendering.

6. Reduce server response time: Ensure your web hosting server responds quickly to requests. Choose a reliable hosting provider and consider upgrading to a higher-performance hosting plan or utilizing server caching techniques to improve response times.

7. Enable GZIP compression: Enable GZIP compression on your web server to reduce file sizes during transmission. Compressed files can be quickly and efficiently transferred between the server and the user's browser, resulting in faster loading times.

8. Optimize database queries: Review and optimize your database queries to improve their efficiency. Proper indexing, query caching, and minimizing unnecessary database calls can significantly improve the performance of database-driven websites.

9. Implement lazy loading: Utilize lazy loading techniques to defer the loading of non-critical resources, such as images or videos, until they are about to come into view. This improves initial page load times and speeds up the perceived performance of your website.

10. Regularly monitor and analyze website performance: Utilize tools like Google PageSpeed Insights, GTmetrix, or WebPageTest to assess your website's performance and identify areas for improvement. Monitor your website's loading speed and other performance metrics to track the impact of optimization efforts.

By implementing these website speed and performance optimization strategies, you can significantly improve the user experience, reduce bounce rates, and enhance your website's search engine rankings. Regularly monitor and fine-tune your optimization efforts to ensure your website continues to perform at its best.

4.2 Mobile Optimization and Responsiveness
Mobile optimization and responsiveness are crucial for delivering a seamless user experience and improving the visibility of your website on mobile devices. Here are some strategies to optimize your website for mobile:

1. Adopt a responsive design: Implement a responsive design approach to ensure your website automatically adjusts and adapts to different screen sizes and resolutions. This ensures that your website is accessible and user-friendly on mobile devices, eliminating the need for separate mobile versions.

2. Use mobile-friendly layouts: Design your web pages with a mobile-first mindset, prioritizing simplicity, readability, and ease of navigation. Use larger fonts, ample white space, and clear calls-to-action to accommodate smaller screens and touch interactions.

3. Optimize page loading speed: Mobile users have shorter attention spans, so it's crucial to optimize your website's loading speed. Compress images, minify CSS and JavaScript, leverage browser caching, and reduce server response time to ensure fast page loading on mobile devices.

4. Implement touch-friendly elements: Make sure your website's buttons, links, and interactive elements are large enough and properly spaced to be easily clickable on touchscreens. Avoid using small, closely spaced elements that can frustrate mobile users.

5. Simplify forms and inputs: Streamline and simplify any forms or input fields on your website to minimize typing and enhance user experience on mobile devices. Use auto-fill or pre-filled options when possible to save users time and effort.

6. Prioritize content and structure: Optimize your website's content for mobile consumption. Prioritize important information, keep paragraphs concise, and use bullet points or subheadings to enhance readability. Break up content into easily scannable sections to accommodate mobile users' shorter attention spans.

7. Test across multiple devices: Ensure your website displays correctly on a variety of mobile devices and screen sizes. Test your website on popular mobile devices and use responsive design testing tools to identify and fix any layout or display issues.

8. Optimize for local search: If your business has a physical location, optimize your website for local search by including location-specific keywords, contact information, and embedding Google Maps for easy navigation. This helps mobile users find and engage with your business.

9. Use mobile-friendly pop-ups: If you use pop-ups on your website, ensure they are mobile-friendly and non-intrusive. Avoid pop-ups that cover the entire screen or are difficult to dismiss on mobile devices, as they can frustrate users.

10. Monitor mobile analytics: Regularly review mobile analytics data to gain insights into user behavior, engagement, and any issues specific to mobile users. Use this data to make informed decisions and continuously optimize your website for mobile performance.

By implementing these mobile optimization and responsiveness strategies, you can provide an excellent user experience on mobile devices and improve your website's visibility in mobile search results. Prioritize mobile-friendliness as mobile usage continues to rise and users increasingly access the web through their smartphones and tablets.

4.3 XML Sitemaps and Robots.txt
XML sitemaps and robots.txt files are important tools for managing and optimizing your website's visibility to search engines. Here's an overview of XML sitemaps and robots.txt files:

1. XML Sitemaps:
  - An XML sitemap is a file that lists all the pages on your website and provides additional information about each page (such as last modified date, priority, etc.).
  - It helps search engine crawlers understand the structure of your website and discover and index your pages more efficiently.
  - XML sitemaps are particularly useful for larger websites with complex structures, websites with dynamic or frequently updated content, and websites with pages that are not easily discovered through internal linking.
  - It's important to regularly update and submit your XML sitemap to search engines to ensure they have the most up-to-date information about your website's pages.

2. Robots.txt:
  - Robots.txt is a text file that tells search engine crawlers which pages or sections of your website they are allowed to crawl and index.
  - It's used to communicate directives to search engine crawlers and instruct them on how to interact with your website.
  - The robots.txt file is placed in the root directory of your website and is accessible at www.yourwebsite.com/robots.txt.
  - You can use robots.txt to allow or disallow crawlers from accessing certain directories or specific pages on your website.
  - It's important to carefully configure your robots.txt file to ensure that search engine crawlers can access and index the pages you want them to, while also protecting sensitive or irrelevant content from being indexed.

Best Practices for XML Sitemaps and Robots.txt:

1. XML Sitemaps:
  - Include all relevant pages: Ensure that your XML sitemap includes all the important pages of your website, including URLs that are not easily discoverable through internal linking.
  - Prioritize important pages: Use the priority attribute to indicate the importance of different pages relative to each other. This helps search engines understand which pages to crawl and index first.
  - Specify last modified date: Include the last modified date for each page in the XML sitemap. This helps search engines determine when to revisit pages for updates.

- Submit to search engines: Submit your XML sitemap to search engines through their respective webmaster tools or search console interfaces.

2. Robots.txt:
  - Use a default robots.txt file: If you don't have specific directives for search engine crawlers, you can use a default robots.txt file that allows all crawlers to access all parts of your website.
  - Disallow sensitive directories: Use the "Disallow" directive to prevent crawlers from accessing directories or specific pages that contain sensitive information or are not intended for indexing.
  - Test your robots.txt file: Use online tools or search engine webmaster tools to test your robots.txt file and ensure it is correctly blocking or allowing access to the intended pages.
  - Regularly review and update: Periodically review and update your robots.txt file as you make changes to your website's structure or content.

By properly utilizing XML sitemaps and robots.txt files, you can improve search engine crawling and indexing of your website, control access to specific pages, and ensure that search engines are aware of your website's structure and content.

4.4 Canonical URLs and Duplicate Content Issues
Canonical URLs and addressing duplicate content issues are important for maintaining a strong SEO presence and preventing any negative impact on search engine rankings. Here's an overview of canonical URLs and duplicate content:

1. Canonical URLs:
  - Canonical URLs are used to indicate the preferred version of a webpage when multiple versions with similar or identical content exist.
  - They help search engines understand which URL should be considered the authoritative or primary version of a page.
  - Canonical URLs are implemented using the "rel=canonical" link element in the HTML head section of a webpage.
  - When multiple URLs have the same or similar content, the canonical URL is specified to inform search engines that it should be treated as the main reference for that content.
  - Canonical URLs consolidate the SEO value and ranking signals of duplicate or similar content onto a single preferred URL, preventing dilution of search engine rankings across multiple versions.

2. Duplicate Content Issues:
  - Duplicate content refers to content that appears on multiple webpages within the same site or across different domains.
  - Search engines strive to provide the most relevant and unique content to users, so they may penalize websites with excessive duplicate content or similar content that offers little added value.
  - Duplicate content can occur due to various reasons, including content replication, session IDs, printer-friendly versions, URL parameters, or syndicated content.
  - Addressing duplicate content is important to avoid confusion for search engines and ensure that the correct version of a page is indexed and ranked.

Best Practices for Canonical URLs and Duplicate Content:

1. Implement canonical URLs:
  - Identify pages with similar or duplicate content and determine the preferred canonical URL for each set of duplicate pages.
  - Add the "rel=canonical" link element in the HTML head section of each duplicate page, specifying the preferred canonical URL.

- Ensure that the canonical URL points to the same domain as the duplicate pages.

2. Use 301 redirects:
   - If duplicate content exists across different domains or subdomains, use 301 redirects to redirect users and search engines to the preferred canonical URL.
   - This ensures that all traffic and ranking signals are consolidated onto the preferred URL.

3. Set preferred versions in Google Search Console:
   - In Google Search Console, you can specify your preferred domain (www or non-www) to indicate which version should be indexed and ranked.
   - You can also use the URL Parameters tool in Search Console to specify how Google should handle URL variations with different parameters.

4. Avoid content replication:
   - Refrain from copying and pasting content from one webpage to another within your own site or from external sources.
   - Instead, focus on creating unique, valuable content that provides additional insights or perspectives.

5. Use appropriate URL structures:
   - Ensure that your website's URL structure is consistent and optimized to avoid unnecessary duplication caused by different URL variations.

6. Canonicalize pagination:
   - If your website has paginated content (e.g., blog posts or product listings spread across multiple pages), use canonical URLs to consolidate the ranking signals onto the main page.

By implementing canonical URLs and addressing duplicate content issues, you can ensure that search engines properly index and rank your preferred content, maintain a strong SEO presence, and avoid any penalties related to duplicate content. Regularly monitor your website for potential duplicate content issues and take necessary actions to resolve them.

4.5 Schema Markup and Structured Data
Schema markup and structured data are powerful tools that provide additional context and information about your website's content to search engines. Here's an overview of schema markup and its benefits:

1. Schema Markup:
   - Schema markup is a standardized vocabulary of tags (or microdata) that can be added to your website's HTML to provide structured data about your content.
   - It helps search engines understand the meaning and context of your content, allowing them to display rich snippets or enhanced search results in the SERPs.
   - Schema markup uses a collection of schemas or categories defined by Schema.org, which is a collaborative project between search engines like Google, Bing, and Yahoo.

2. Benefits of Schema Markup:
   - Enhanced search results: Schema markup can enable rich snippets, which provide additional information, such as star ratings, reviews, pricing, event details, and more, directly in the search results. This helps your website stand out and increases click-through rates.

- Improved search engine understanding: By providing structured data, search engines can better understand the content and context of your website. This can lead to improved relevancy and visibility in search results.
- Voice search optimization: Structured data can also help optimize your website for voice search, as voice assistants rely on structured data to provide relevant answers to user queries.
- Increased visibility for local businesses: Schema markup can include location-specific information, such as business address, phone number, and opening hours, which can improve local search visibility and help users find your business more easily.
- More targeted results: Schema markup allows you to provide specific details about your content, such as product information, recipes, events, and more. This enables search engines to deliver more targeted results to users.

Best Practices for Schema Markup:

1. Choose relevant schema types: Identify the most appropriate schema types for your content. Schema.org offers a wide range of schema types, including articles, reviews, products, events, recipes, and more. Select the schema types that best describe your content.

2. Implement structured data on key pages: Focus on implementing structured data on pages that are most relevant to your business or have the potential to display rich snippets in search results, such as product pages, review pages, or event pages.

3. Follow schema guidelines: Follow the guidelines provided by Schema.org for each schema type you use. Ensure that you accurately represent your content and provide the required properties and values.

4. Test your structured data: Use the structured data testing tools provided by search engines, such as Google's Structured Data Testing Tool or the Rich Results Test, to validate and verify your schema markup. Fix any errors or warnings that are identified.

5. Monitor and update structured data: Regularly monitor your website's structured data to ensure it remains accurate and up to date. Make updates as needed when you add new content or modify existing content.

By implementing schema markup and structured data on your website, you can provide search engines with additional information about your content, enhance search results, and improve the visibility and click-through rates of your web pages. It's an effective way to make your website stand out in search results and deliver a better user experience.

4.6 URL Structure and Redirects
URL structure and redirects play a crucial role in search engine optimization and user experience. Here's an overview of best practices for URL structure and redirects:

1. URL Structure:
- Keep URLs descriptive and readable: Use meaningful words and phrases in your URLs that accurately describe the content of the page. Avoid using random strings of numbers or irrelevant characters.
- Use hyphens to separate words: Use hyphens (-) to separate words in the URL, as search engines recognize hyphens as word separators. Avoid using underscores (_) or spaces.
- Keep URLs concise: Aim for shorter URLs that are easy to read and remember. Long and complex URLs can be confusing to users and search engines.

- Include target keywords: If relevant and natural, include target keywords in the URL to provide additional context to search engines and users.
  - Structure URLs logically: Organize your URLs in a hierarchical structure that reflects the information architecture of your website. Use subdirectories to categorize content.

2. Redirects:
  - Use 301 redirects for permanent redirects: If you change the URL of a page permanently, use a 301 redirect to redirect users and search engines to the new URL. This ensures that the authority and rankings of the old URL are transferred to the new one.
  - Implement redirects for broken or deleted pages: If you delete or remove a page from your website, redirect the URL to a relevant page using a 301 redirect. This prevents users and search engines from encountering broken links and helps maintain the flow of traffic.
  - Avoid redirect chains: Minimize the number of redirects between the original URL and the final destination. Redirect chains can slow down page load times and negatively impact SEO.
  - Update internal links: After implementing redirects, update internal links within your website to point to the new URLs. This ensures a smooth user experience and avoids unnecessary redirects.
  - Monitor redirect loops and errors: Regularly check for any redirect loops or errors that may occur. Use tools like Google Search Console to identify and resolve any issues.

Best Practices for URL Structure and Redirects:

1. Plan your URL structure in advance: Establish a clear URL structure during the initial website planning phase. This helps create a logical hierarchy and makes it easier to maintain and manage URLs in the long run.

2. Use canonical URLs for duplicate content: When multiple URLs have similar or identical content, implement canonical tags to specify the preferred URL. This helps search engines understand the canonical version and avoid duplicate content issues.

3. Implement redirects for URL changes: If you need to change the URL of a page, set up a 301 redirect to redirect users and search engines to the new URL. This ensures a smooth transition and prevents the loss of rankings and traffic.

4. Monitor and fix broken links: Regularly check for broken links on your website using tools like Google Search Console or third-party link checkers. Fix any broken links by implementing redirects or updating the links to point to valid pages.

5. Be consistent with URL structure: Maintain consistency in your URL structure throughout the website. Use consistent naming conventions and avoid unnecessary variations to create a user-friendly experience.

By following these best practices for URL structure and redirects, you can improve the usability and accessibility of your website, maintain SEO rankings, and ensure a positive user experience. Regularly monitor your URLs, implement redirects when necessary, and keep your URL structure organized and descriptive.

Chapter 5:
Content Creation and Optimization

5.1 Creating High-Quality and Engaging Content
Creating high-quality and engaging content is essential for attracting and retaining your target audience. Here are some key practices to consider:

1. Understand your target audience: Research and understand your target audience's needs, preferences, and pain points. Tailor your content to address their specific interests and provide value.

2. Develop a content strategy: Plan your content in advance and align it with your business goals. Define the topics, formats, and channels that will resonate with your audience. Consider creating a content calendar to stay organized and consistent.

3. Focus on originality and uniqueness: Aim to create original and unique content that stands out from the competition. Offer fresh perspectives, unique insights, and innovative ideas to captivate your audience.

4. Provide valuable and actionable information: Deliver content that provides practical and actionable information. Address your audience's challenges and provide solutions, tips, tutorials, case studies, or industry insights that they can apply in their own lives or businesses.

5. Use a variety of content formats: Experiment with different content formats, such as articles, blog posts, videos, infographics, podcasts, and interactive content. Cater to different learning preferences and engage your audience with a diverse range of formats.

6. Incorporate visuals and multimedia: Visual elements, such as images, videos, charts, and infographics, can enhance the appeal and effectiveness of your content. Use relevant visuals to illustrate concepts, break up text, and make your content more visually appealing.

7. Craft compelling headlines and introductions: Grab your audience's attention with compelling headlines and introductions. Clearly communicate the value and relevance of your content, and entice readers to continue reading or watching.

8. Write in a clear and concise manner: Use plain language and avoid jargon or complex technical terms. Keep your sentences and paragraphs concise, making your content easy to read and understand.

9. Incorporate storytelling techniques: Weave storytelling elements into your content to make it more relatable and engaging. Use anecdotes, personal experiences, or customer success stories to create an emotional connection with your audience.

10. Encourage interaction and engagement: Prompt your audience to engage with your content through comments, social media shares, likes, and discussions. Respond to comments and engage in conversations to foster a sense of community and build relationships with your audience.

11. Continuously optimize and update your content: Regularly review and update your existing content to ensure its accuracy, relevance, and freshness. Monitor analytics to understand which types of content perform well and adjust your strategy accordingly.

Remember, creating high-quality and engaging content requires a deep understanding of your audience's needs and preferences. Continuously adapt and refine your content strategy based on audience feedback, analytics data, and industry trends to ensure that you consistently deliver valuable and captivating content.

5.2 Incorporating Keywords Naturally in Content

Incorporating keywords naturally in your content is crucial for optimizing your website for search engines. Here are some tips to help you effectively incorporate keywords while maintaining a natural flow:

1. Keyword research: Start by conducting keyword research to identify relevant keywords and phrases that align with your content and target audience. Use tools like Google Keyword Planner, SEMrush, or Moz Keyword Explorer to find keywords with a good balance of search volume and competition.

2. Strategic placement: Place your primary keyword in strategic locations within your content, such as the title tag, heading tags (H1, H2), meta description, and the first paragraph of your content. These are important areas that search engines consider when determining the relevance of your content.

3. Use variations and synonyms: Avoid overusing the exact same keyword throughout your content. Instead, incorporate variations and synonyms of your primary keyword to add diversity and make your content more natural and reader-friendly. This helps capture different search queries and improves the overall user experience.

4. Write for readers, not just search engines: While it's important to optimize your content for search engines, remember that your primary audience is human readers. Focus on creating valuable, informative, and engaging content that provides a great user experience. If your content is valuable and engaging, it will naturally include relevant keywords.

5. Maintain a natural flow: Ensure that your keywords fit naturally within your sentences and paragraphs. Avoid "keyword stuffing," which is the excessive and unnatural use of keywords. It not only makes your content difficult to read but can also lead to penalties from search engines. Use keywords sparingly and only when they naturally fit into the context of your content.

6. Create comprehensive content: Rather than focusing solely on individual keywords, aim to create comprehensive content that covers a topic in-depth. This naturally incorporates related keywords and provides more value to your readers. Search engines also appreciate comprehensive content that addresses various aspects of a topic.

7. Use long-tail keywords: Long-tail keywords are longer and more specific phrases that target a narrower audience. They are often less competitive and can help you rank higher for specific searches. Incorporate long-tail keywords naturally into your content to capture the attention of users with specific search queries.

8. Regularly review and update your content: Stay up to date with keyword trends and changes in search behavior. Regularly review and update your content to ensure that your keywords remain relevant and aligned with current search queries.

Remember, the goal is to create high-quality content that resonates with your audience while incorporating relevant keywords. By striking a balance between optimization and natural writing, you can improve your search engine visibility and provide a positive user experience.

5.3 Optimizing Content Length and Readability
Optimizing content length and readability is important for engaging your audience and improving search engine visibility. Here are some tips to help you optimize content length and readability:

1. Understand your audience: Consider the preferences and needs of your target audience. Some topics may require more in-depth and lengthy content, while others may benefit from shorter and concise pieces. Research your audience to determine their preferences.

2. Focus on quality over quantity: Rather than aiming for a specific word count, prioritize the quality of your content. Provide valuable and comprehensive information that addresses the needs of your audience. This helps establish your authority and keeps readers engaged.

3. Use clear and concise language: Write in a clear and concise manner to make your content easy to understand. Avoid jargon, complex sentences, and unnecessary technical terms. Break down complex concepts into simple, digestible chunks.

4. Use headings and subheadings: Structure your content with headings and subheadings to improve readability. This helps readers scan your content and find information quickly. Use descriptive headings that accurately reflect the content under each section.

5. Utilize bullet points and lists: Break down information using bullet points or numbered lists. This format makes content more scannable and helps readers grasp key points without overwhelming them with lengthy paragraphs.

6. Incorporate visuals: Include relevant images, infographics, or videos to enhance the visual appeal of your content. Visuals can break up text, convey information more effectively, and engage readers.

7. Pay attention to paragraph length: Keep paragraphs relatively short to avoid overwhelming readers. Aim for 3-4 sentences per paragraph, making it easier for readers to follow along and digest the content.

8. Use white space effectively: Don't overcrowd your content. Leave adequate white space between paragraphs and sections to give readers breathing room and make the content visually appealing.

9. Proofread and edit: Ensure your content is free from grammar and spelling errors. Proofread carefully, and if possible, have someone else review your content for a fresh perspective. Clear and error-free content enhances readability.

10. Test readability tools: Use readability tools like the Flesch-Kincaid Readability Test or the Gunning Fog Index to assess the readability level of your content. Aim for a readability level that matches your target audience.

11. Break up long content into series or chapters: If your content is lengthy, consider breaking it up into a series of articles or chapters. This allows readers to consume the information in smaller, more manageable chunks.

Remember, every piece of content is unique, and the optimal length may vary depending on the topic, audience, and platform. Prioritize delivering valuable information in a readable and engaging manner. By focusing on quality, clarity, and readability, you can optimize your content for both readers and search engines.

5.4 Incorporating Multimedia Elements

Incorporating multimedia elements into your content can enhance user engagement and make your content more visually appealing. Here are some tips for effectively incorporating multimedia elements:

1. Images and graphics: Use relevant images, graphics, or illustrations to support your content and make it visually appealing. Choose high-quality visuals that are relevant to your topic and help convey your message effectively.

2. Infographics: Create informative and visually appealing infographics to present data, statistics, or complex concepts in a visually appealing and easy-to-understand format. Infographics can help break down information into digestible chunks and increase shareability.

3. Videos: Incorporate videos to provide demonstrations, tutorials, or interviews related to your content. Videos can be engaging and help users grasp concepts more effectively. Host your videos on platforms like YouTube or Vimeo and embed them in your content.

4. Slideshows and presentations: Use slideshows or presentations to present information in a visually appealing way. Tools like SlideShare or Google Slides can help you create interactive and informative slideshows.

5. Audio clips or podcasts: If relevant to your content, include audio clips or podcasts to provide additional information or interviews. Audio content can be a great way to engage users who prefer auditory learning.

6. Interactive elements: Consider incorporating interactive elements such as quizzes, surveys, or interactive maps to make your content more engaging and encourage user participation. Interactive elements can enhance user experience and increase time spent on your content.

7. GIFs and animations: Use GIFs or short animations to add a touch of humor, demonstrate a process, or highlight specific points in your content. GIFs can capture attention and make your content more dynamic.

8. Social media embeds: Embed social media posts, such as tweets or Instagram photos, that are relevant to your content. This can provide social proof, encourage sharing, and add an interactive element to your content.

9. Visual diagrams and charts: Incorporate visual diagrams or charts to present complex information or data in a simplified and easy-to-understand format. Visual representations can help users grasp information quickly.

10. Interactive maps or timelines: Use interactive maps or timelines to showcase location-specific information or historical events related to your content. This can enhance the user experience and provide a visually appealing way to present information.

When incorporating multimedia elements, ensure they are relevant, enhance the understanding of your content, and align with your target audience's preferences. Balance the use of multimedia with the overall readability and accessibility of your content. By incorporating multimedia elements strategically, you can make your content more engaging and memorable for your audience.

5.5 User-Generated Content and its Impact on SEO
User-generated content (UGC) refers to any content that is created and shared by users or customers, such as reviews, comments, testimonials, social media posts, and forum discussions. UGC can have a significant impact on SEO. Here's how:

1. Increased engagement and social proof: UGC encourages user engagement and interaction with your website or brand. When users actively participate by leaving reviews, comments, or sharing their experiences, it creates social proof, indicating to search engines and other users that your website is valuable and trustworthy.

2. Fresh and relevant content: UGC adds fresh and unique content to your website. Search engines value regularly updated content, and UGC helps you consistently add new content without solely relying on your own efforts. User-generated reviews, for example, can provide valuable insights and information to potential customers and improve your website's relevancy in search results.

3. Long-tail keywords and diverse language: UGC often includes a variety of long-tail keywords and natural language that users use when discussing products, services, or experiences. This can broaden your website's keyword reach and attract more organic traffic from specific search queries.

4. Improved search rankings: Search engines consider user-generated content as a measure of website quality and relevance. Positive user reviews and high engagement can contribute to higher search rankings. Additionally, UGC often generates more backlinks and social media shares, further boosting your website's visibility and authority.

5. Enhanced trust and credibility: User-generated content, particularly positive reviews and testimonials, builds trust and credibility among potential customers. When search engines see positive sentiment and engagement around your brand, it increases the likelihood of higher rankings and improved click-through rates.

To leverage the impact of user-generated content on SEO, consider the following tips:

- Encourage and facilitate user-generated content: Actively encourage your customers to leave reviews, testimonials, and comments. Provide clear opportunities and incentives for them to engage with your brand and share their experiences.

- Moderate and respond to UGC: Monitor and moderate user-generated content to ensure it aligns with your brand values and guidelines. Respond to comments and engage with users to show that you value their input and feedback.

- Showcase UGC on your website: Display user-generated content prominently on your website. This can include testimonials on product pages, user reviews, or a dedicated section for customer stories. This not only enhances the user experience but also reinforces the positive impact of UGC on SEO.

- Utilize UGC in social media and marketing campaigns: Incorporate user-generated content in your social media strategy and marketing campaigns. Share positive reviews, customer photos, or user stories to build brand loyalty and encourage further engagement.

- Monitor and analyze UGC: Regularly analyze user-generated content to gain insights into customer sentiment, preferences, and trends. This data can inform your SEO strategy, content creation, and overall business decisions.

Remember, user-generated content can be a powerful tool for SEO and brand building. By actively encouraging and leveraging UGC, you can enhance your website's visibility, trustworthiness, and engagement, leading to improved search rankings and increased organic traffic.

Chapter 6:
Off-Page Optimization and Link Building

6.1 Importance of Off-Page Optimization
Off-page optimization plays a crucial role in improving the visibility and authority of your website in search engine rankings. Here are some key reasons why off-page optimization is important:

1. Building backlinks: Off-page optimization involves acquiring high-quality backlinks from other reputable websites. Backlinks act as votes of confidence from other websites, indicating that your content is valuable and trustworthy. Search engines consider backlinks as a major ranking factor, and websites with a strong backlink profile tend to rank higher in search results.

2. Increasing website authority: Off-page optimization helps to establish your website as an authoritative source within your industry or niche. When other reputable websites link to your content, it signals to search engines that your website is valuable and relevant. This improves your website's overall authority, which can lead to higher search rankings.

3. Enhancing online reputation: Off-page optimization includes activities such as online reputation management and brand building. By actively managing your online presence and engaging with your audience on social media and other platforms, you can build a positive reputation and establish trust with potential customers. A strong online reputation can attract more visitors to your website and increase user engagement.

4. Increasing organic traffic: When your website has a strong off-page optimization strategy, it can result in higher organic traffic. As your search engine rankings improve, more users are likely to discover and visit your website. This can lead to increased brand exposure, higher click-through rates, and ultimately, more qualified leads and conversions.

5. Expanding your online reach: Off-page optimization allows you to extend your online reach beyond your website. By participating in guest blogging, influencer collaborations, social media engagement, and other off-site activities, you can tap into new audiences and attract visitors who may not have been aware of your website otherwise. This helps to increase brand visibility and generate more traffic.

6. Staying competitive in the digital landscape: In today's highly competitive digital landscape, off-page optimization is essential for staying ahead of your competitors. By actively building backlinks, engaging with influencers, and establishing a strong online presence, you can differentiate your website from others in your industry and attract more attention from search engines and users.

To effectively implement off-page optimization strategies, consider the following best practices:

- Develop a backlink acquisition strategy: Identify authoritative websites and relevant industry influencers to target for backlinks. Create valuable content that others will want to link to and engage in outreach activities to promote your content.

- Foster relationships with influencers and industry leaders: Engage with influencers and industry leaders through social media, guest blogging, or collaborative projects. Building relationships can lead to opportunities for guest posting, mentions, and partnerships that can enhance your online presence.

- Monitor and manage your online reputation: Regularly monitor your brand mentions and online reviews. Respond promptly to customer feedback and address any negative comments to maintain a positive online reputation.

- Leverage social media: Actively engage with your audience on social media platforms. Share your content, participate in relevant conversations, and build a community of loyal followers who can amplify your brand's reach.

- Monitor and analyze your off-page efforts: Use tools and analytics to track the performance of your backlinks, social media engagement, and other off-page activities. This data will help you evaluate the effectiveness of your strategies and make informed decisions for future optimization.

By implementing a well-rounded off-page optimization strategy, you can enhance your website's visibility, authority, and online reputation, leading to increased organic traffic, higher search rankings, and improved competitiveness in the digital landscape.

6.2 Building High-Quality Backlinks
Building high-quality backlinks is crucial for off-page optimization and improving your website's search engine rankings. Here are some effective strategies for building high-quality backlinks:

1. Create valuable and shareable content: Produce high-quality content that provides value to your target audience. When your content is informative, well-researched, and engaging, it increases the chances of other websites linking to it naturally.

2. Guest blogging: Reach out to authoritative websites or blogs in your industry and offer to write guest posts. Guest blogging allows you to showcase your expertise, reach a new audience, and earn backlinks from reputable sources. Ensure that your guest posts provide valuable insights and are relevant to the host website's audience.

3. Resource link building: Create comprehensive and informative resources on your website, such as guides, tutorials, or industry reports. Promote these resources to relevant websites and ask them to link to your content as a valuable resource for their audience.

4. Broken link building: Identify broken links on other websites that are related to your industry or content. Reach out to the website owners, notify them about the broken link, and suggest your content as a replacement. This approach provides value to the website owner by helping them fix broken links and gives you an opportunity to earn a backlink.

5. Influencer collaborations: Collaborate with influencers or industry experts who have a strong online presence and a significant following. Engage with them through interviews, joint content creation, or partnerships. When influencers share or mention your content, it can lead to valuable backlinks and increased exposure.

6. Social media promotion: Share your content on social media platforms to increase its visibility and encourage others to link to it. Engage with your audience and relevant communities by participating in discussions, answering questions, and sharing insights. This can attract attention and potential backlinks from social media users.

7. Participate in industry forums and communities: Engage in relevant online forums, discussion boards, and communities where your target audience gathers. Share your expertise, provide helpful insights, and include a link to your website when relevant. This can generate backlinks and establish your credibility in the industry.

8. Build relationships with journalists and publishers: Develop relationships with journalists, bloggers, and publishers who cover topics related to your industry. Provide them with valuable information, data, or expert insights that can contribute to their articles. This can lead to mentions and backlinks in their content.

9. Monitor and reclaim brand mentions: Use tools to monitor brand mentions and unlinked references to your website. Reach out to the authors or website owners and kindly request them to add a backlink to your website for proper attribution.

10. Focus on quality over quantity: Prioritize acquiring high-quality backlinks from authoritative and relevant websites. A few high-quality backlinks from trusted sources are more valuable than numerous low-quality backlinks.

Remember, when building backlinks, it's important to maintain ethical practices and follow search engine guidelines. Avoid engaging in link schemes, buying or exchanging links, or using manipulative tactics that can harm your website's reputation and rankings.

Building high-quality backlinks takes time and effort, but the results can significantly enhance your website's visibility, authority, and search engine rankings.

6.3 Guest Blogging and Influencer Outreach
Guest blogging and influencer outreach are effective strategies for building backlinks, expanding your online presence, and reaching a wider audience. Here's how you can effectively leverage guest blogging and influencer outreach:

Guest Blogging:

1. Identify relevant blogs: Research and identify reputable blogs in your industry or niche that accept guest posts. Look for blogs that have an engaged audience and align with your target market.

2. Study their guidelines: Before reaching out, carefully read and understand the guest blogging guidelines provided by the target blogs. Follow their instructions regarding content topics, word count, formatting, and submission process.

3. Craft high-quality content: Create informative, well-researched, and engaging content that adds value to the readers of the target blog. Tailor your content to fit the blog's style and audience. Focus on providing unique insights, practical tips, or thought-provoking perspectives.

4. Pitch your guest post: Write a compelling and personalized pitch to the blog's editor or content manager. Explain why your guest post would be a valuable addition to their blog and highlight the

benefits it can offer to their audience. Share relevant samples of your previous work to showcase your writing skills and expertise.

5. Follow editorial guidelines: Once your guest post is accepted, adhere to the blog's editorial guidelines regarding formatting, links, and any specific requirements. Craft your post with attention to detail, including a catchy headline, subheadings, and relevant images if allowed.

6. Promote your guest post: After your guest post is published, promote it on your own website, social media channels, and email newsletters. Engage with readers' comments and questions to foster discussions. This helps to increase the visibility of your guest post and drive traffic back to your own website.

Influencer Outreach:

1. Identify relevant influencers: Identify influencers in your industry who have a significant following and engage with your target audience. Look for influencers who align with your brand values and have a genuine interest in your content or products.

2. Engage with their content: Start by engaging with their content through likes, comments, and shares. Build a genuine connection by adding value to their discussions and demonstrating your expertise or appreciation for their work.

3. Personalized outreach: Reach out to influencers with a personalized message expressing why you admire their work and how your collaboration can be mutually beneficial. Be clear about your intentions, whether it's a guest blog contribution, a collaboration on social media, or a joint content creation project.

4. Provide value: Offer something valuable to the influencer, such as unique content, research data, or an exclusive opportunity to collaborate. Emphasize how your collaboration can benefit their audience and enhance their own brand.

5. Build relationships: Cultivate relationships with influencers by maintaining regular communication, sharing their content, and promoting their work. Collaboration should be a long-term strategy, and nurturing relationships can lead to further opportunities in the future.

6. Measure and track results: Monitor the impact of your influencer outreach efforts by tracking metrics such as website traffic, social media engagement, and backlinks generated. Adjust your strategies based on the results and continuously refine your influencer outreach approach.

Remember, both guest blogging and influencer outreach require building authentic relationships and providing value to the target blogs or influencers. By consistently producing high-quality content and fostering meaningful connections, you can leverage these strategies to expand your reach, build authority, and drive traffic to your website.

6.4 Social Media Signals and SEO
Social media signals refer to the impact of social media engagement and activity on search engine optimization (SEO). While social media signals themselves may not have a direct impact on search engine rankings, they can indirectly influence SEO in the following ways:

1. Increased website visibility: When your content is shared, liked, and commented on social media platforms, it can lead to increased visibility and exposure. This can result in more people discovering your content and linking to it from their websites, which can positively impact your website's SEO.

2. Generating backlinks: Social media can serve as a distribution channel for your content, making it more likely to be seen and shared by others. When your content is shared on social media, it increases the chances of others linking to it from their websites or blogs, thus generating valuable backlinks that contribute to your website's authority and rankings.

3. Improved brand awareness and reputation: Active engagement on social media platforms can help build your brand's visibility and reputation. When people are aware of and trust your brand, they are more likely to search for it by name, which can lead to higher search volumes and improved organic rankings.

4. Increased traffic and user engagement: Social media platforms can drive significant amounts of traffic to your website. When users visit your website from social media, spend time engaging with your content, and perform desired actions (such as sharing or making a purchase), it signals to search engines that your website is valuable and relevant, potentially leading to improved search rankings.

5. Social media profiles in search results: Search engines often index social media profiles, and these profiles can appear in search results for brand-related queries. Having active and optimized social media profiles can enhance your online presence and provide additional opportunities for users to discover and engage with your brand.

To optimize the impact of social media signals on your SEO efforts, consider the following tips:

- Create high-quality and shareable content: Produce valuable and engaging content that resonates with your target audience. The more people find your content useful and share-worthy, the higher the chances of it gaining traction on social media and attracting backlinks.

- Optimize your social media profiles: Ensure that your social media profiles are complete, consistent, and aligned with your brand identity. Use relevant keywords in your profiles and include links to your website or important landing pages.

- Encourage social sharing: Make it easy for users to share your content on social media by incorporating social sharing buttons on your website and blog posts. Encourage readers to share your content if they find it valuable or insightful.

- Engage with your audience: Actively engage with your followers and audience on social media platforms. Respond to comments, answer questions, and participate in relevant discussions. This helps build relationships, encourage more interactions, and increase the visibility of your brand.

- Monitor and analyze social media metrics: Use social media analytics tools to track the performance of your social media efforts. Monitor metrics such as engagement, reach, shares, and click-through rates to gain insights into what resonates with your audience and adjust your social media strategy accordingly.

While social media signals are not direct ranking factors, they can significantly impact your SEO efforts by driving traffic, generating backlinks, and improving brand awareness. By leveraging social media effectively, you can enhance your overall online presence and contribute to the success of your SEO strategy.

6.5 Online Directories and Local Citations
Online directories and local citations play a crucial role in local SEO, helping businesses improve their visibility in local search results. Here's how they work and their impact on SEO:

1. What are online directories and local citations?
Online directories are websites that list businesses and their contact information, such as name, address, phone number (NAP), and website URL. They serve as online directories for specific industries or geographical locations. Local citations, on the other hand, refer to the mentions of your business's NAP information on various online platforms, including directories, review sites, social media profiles, and more.

2. Importance of online directories and local citations for SEO:
- Improved local visibility: Online directories and local citations help search engines understand the relevance and location of your business. When search engines see consistent NAP information across multiple directories and platforms, it strengthens the trustworthiness and legitimacy of your business, improving your chances of ranking higher in local search results.

- Increased website authority: When your business is listed in reputable directories and receives citations from authoritative sources, it can positively impact your website's authority and credibility. Search engines consider backlinks from directories and citations as a signal of trustworthiness, which can contribute to higher search rankings.

- Enhanced online reputation: Online directories often include user reviews and ratings. Positive reviews can enhance your online reputation and attract more customers. Additionally, user-generated content like reviews can also contribute to SEO by adding unique and relevant content related to your business.

3. Best practices for leveraging online directories and local citations:
- Ensure NAP consistency: Maintain consistent and accurate NAP information across all online directories and platforms. Inconsistencies can confuse search engines and users, leading to lower search rankings and a negative user experience.

- Choose reputable directories: Focus on authoritative directories that are relevant to your industry and location. Consider well-known directories like Google My Business, Yelp, Yellow Pages, and industry-specific directories. Listing your business in directories that have a strong online presence and good domain authority can have a more significant impact on your SEO.

- Optimize directory listings: Provide complete and detailed information about your business, including a compelling description, relevant keywords, business hours, photos, and website links. The more information you provide, the easier it is for search engines and users to understand and engage with your business.

- Monitor and manage your listings: Regularly monitor your online directory listings for accuracy and any user-generated content like reviews or comments. Respond promptly and professionally to reviews, both positive and negative, to demonstrate your commitment to customer satisfaction.

- Build citations from reputable sources: Seek opportunities to acquire citations from authoritative sources such as local news websites, industry associations, and local business directories. These high-quality citations can boost your website's authority and visibility in local search results.

4. Local SEO tools for managing online directories and citations:
Several tools can assist you in managing your online directories and local citations effectively. Examples include Moz Local, Yet, Bright Local, and White spark. These tools provide features like citation monitoring, review management, and NAP consistency checks.

By optimizing your presence in online directories, ensuring NAP consistency, and actively managing your local citations, you can enhance your local SEO efforts and improve your visibility in local search results. It's important to stay proactive in monitoring and maintaining your online directory listings to ensure accurate and up-to-date information for both search engines and potential customers.

Chapter 7:
User Experience and SEO

7.1 Website Navigation and Structure
Website navigation and structure are crucial aspects of user experience (UX) and search engine optimization (SEO). A well-designed website navigation helps users find information easily, improves engagement, and encourages them to explore more pages on your site. Additionally, a clear and organized website structure enables search engines to crawl and index your site effectively. Here are some best practices for website navigation and structure:

1. Clear and intuitive navigation menu: Design a clear and user-friendly navigation menu that is easily accessible and prominently displayed on your website. Use descriptive and concise labels for menu items, and organize them logically to guide users to different sections or categories of your site.

2. Logical hierarchy and categories: Create a logical hierarchy for your website content, with broader categories and subcategories that reflect the organization of information. This helps users understand the structure of your website and navigate through different sections with ease.

3. Consistent navigation across pages: Maintain consistent navigation elements throughout your website, including header menus, footer menus, or sidebars. Consistency in navigation ensures that users can easily find their way around, regardless of which page they are on.

4. Breadcrumb navigation: Implement breadcrumb navigation to provide users with a clear path back to higher-level pages. Breadcrumbs help users understand their current location within the site's structure and can improve navigation and user experience.

5. User-friendly URLs: Create user-friendly URLs that are descriptive and easy to understand. Use keywords relevant to the page content in the URL structure, and avoid using long or complex URLs that can confuse users and search engines.

6. Internal linking: Use internal links within your website to connect related pages and guide users to relevant content. Internal linking not only aids navigation but also helps search engines discover and crawl your site more effectively.

7. Mobile-friendly navigation: Ensure that your website's navigation is optimized for mobile devices. Mobile users should be able to easily access and navigate your site on smaller screens without any usability issues.

8. Site map: Include a sitemap on your website to provide a hierarchical overview of your site's structure. A sitemap helps search engines understand the organization of your content and crawl your site more efficiently.

9. User testing and feedback: Conduct user testing to gather feedback on your website navigation and structure. Analyze user behavior, observe their navigation patterns, and make improvements based on their feedback to enhance usability.

10. SEO considerations: When designing your website structure, keep SEO in mind. Ensure that important pages are easily accessible within a few clicks, and prioritize content that you want to rank well in search results. Optimize your navigation labels and URLs with relevant keywords to improve search engine visibility.

By implementing these best practices, you can create a user-friendly website navigation and structure that enhances the user experience, helps visitors find information efficiently, and improves your website's SEO performance.

7.2 User-Friendly Design and Layout

User-friendly design and layout are essential for creating a positive user experience (UX) on your website. A user-friendly design helps visitors navigate your site easily, find information quickly, and engage with your content effectively. Here are some key considerations for designing a user-friendly website:

1. Intuitive and organized layout: Create a clean and organized layout that allows users to easily understand the structure of your website. Use visual hierarchy to prioritize important elements, such as headlines, subheadings, and calls to action, making it clear what users should focus on.

2. Responsive design: Ensure that your website is responsive and adapts to different screen sizes and devices. A responsive design provides a consistent and optimal experience for users, regardless of whether they are accessing your site on a desktop, tablet, or mobile device.

3. Readable typography: Choose fonts and font sizes that are easy to read on various devices and screen sizes. Use sufficient line spacing and contrast between text and background to enhance readability. Avoid using excessive decorative fonts that may impair readability.

4. Clear and concise content: Present your content in a clear and concise manner, using short paragraphs, bullet points, and headings to break up text. Use plain language that is easy for users to understand, avoiding jargon or technical terms when possible.

5. Visual elements and multimedia: Incorporate visual elements such as images, videos, and infographics to enhance your content and engage users. However, ensure that visual elements are optimized for fast loading times and do not overpower or distract from the main message.

6. Consistent branding: Maintain consistent branding elements, such as your logo, color scheme, and typography, throughout your website. Consistency helps users recognize and connect with your brand, enhancing trust and familiarity.

7. Easy navigation: Design an intuitive and easy-to-use navigation menu that allows users to navigate your website effortlessly. Use descriptive labels for menu items and provide clear links to important pages or sections of your site.

8. Call-to-action (CTA) placement: Strategically place prominent and compelling CTAs throughout your website to guide users towards desired actions, such as signing up for a newsletter or making a purchase. Use contrasting colors and persuasive copy to make CTAs stand out.

9. White space and breathing room: Incorporate ample white space between elements to provide visual clarity and improve readability. White space helps users focus on important content and prevents the design from appearing cluttered.

10. User testing and feedback: Conduct user testing to gather feedback on your website's design and layout. Observe how users interact with your site, identify any pain points or confusion, and make necessary improvements based on user feedback.

Remember, user-friendly design is a continuous process. Regularly analyze user behavior, track metrics, and iterate on your design to improve the overall user experience. By prioritizing usability, readability, and intuitive design, you can create a website that visitors find easy to navigate and enjoyable to interact with.

7.3 Mobile User Experience
Mobile user experience (UX) is critical in today's digital landscape as an increasing number of users access websites and applications on mobile devices. Creating a seamless and optimized mobile experience is essential for engaging mobile users and maximizing conversions. Here are some key considerations for enhancing mobile UX:

1. Responsive design: Ensure your website or application is built with a responsive design that adapts to different screen sizes and orientations. This allows content to be displayed properly and ensures a consistent experience across various mobile devices.

2. Fast loading times: Mobile users have limited patience for slow-loading websites. Optimize your site's performance by minimizing file sizes, leveraging caching techniques, and optimizing server responses. Aim for fast page load times to keep mobile users engaged.

3. Streamlined content: Simplify your content for mobile screens by focusing on the most essential information. Use concise headlines, shorter paragraphs, bullet points, and visual elements to make content scannable and digestible on smaller screens.

4. Mobile-friendly navigation: Design a navigation menu that is optimized for mobile devices. Utilize hamburger menus, collapsible sections, or slide-out panels to keep the navigation clean and unobtrusive. Ensure that menu items are easily tappable and accessible with a thumb.

5. Touch-friendly elements: Make sure interactive elements such as buttons, links, and form fields are large enough and properly spaced to accommodate finger taps. Avoid placing clickable elements too close together to prevent accidental taps.

6. Clear call-to-action (CTA): Place prominent and easily identifiable CTAs on mobile pages. Use contrasting colors, concise text, and a clear design to encourage users to take desired actions.

7. Mobile forms optimization: Simplify and streamline forms for mobile users. Minimize the number of required fields, use auto-fill and validation features, and optimize the keyboard input experience. Utilize input types appropriate for mobile devices, such as date pickers or number keyboards.

8. Avoid intrusive pop-ups: Mobile screens have limited space, so avoid intrusive pop-ups that hinder the user experience. If using pop-ups, ensure they are easily dismissible and do not cover the main content or disrupt the user flow.

9. Visual hierarchy: Use visual cues, such as contrasting colors, size, and placement, to establish a clear visual hierarchy on mobile screens. Highlight important elements and key information to guide users' attention and facilitate easy scanning.

10. Mobile testing and optimization: Regularly test your website or application on various mobile devices and screen sizes to identify any issues or usability challenges. Continuously optimize and improve the mobile experience based on user feedback and behavior data.

By prioritizing mobile UX and following these best practices, you can create a mobile-friendly experience that engages and delights users, leading to increased engagement, conversions, and overall satisfaction with your website or application.

7.4 Website Accessibility and SEO
Website accessibility and SEO (Search Engine Optimization) are two separate but interconnected aspects of web development and online presence. Here's an overview of each topic and how they relate to each other:

1. Website Accessibility:
Website accessibility refers to the inclusive design and development of websites to ensure they can be used and accessed by all individuals, including those with disabilities. It aims to remove barriers and provide equal access to information, functionality, and services for people with diverse abilities.

Key aspects of website accessibility include:

- Text alternatives: Providing alternative text descriptions for non-text content, such as images, for screen readers and assistive technologies.
- Keyboard accessibility: Ensuring that all functionality and interactive elements can be accessed and operated using a keyboard alone, without relying on a mouse.
- Color contrast: Maintaining sufficient contrast between foreground and background colors to ensure readability for individuals with visual impairments.
- Proper heading structure: Structuring web content using semantic HTML headings (h1, h2, etc.) to facilitate navigation and understanding for screen readers.
- Navigation and focus indicators: Ensuring clear and logical navigation pathways and providing visual indicators to highlight the currently focused element for keyboard users.
- Captions and transcripts: Providing captions or transcripts for audio and video content to assist users with hearing impairments.

2. SEO (Search Engine Optimization):
SEO involves optimizing a website to improve its visibility and ranking in search engine results pages. The goal is to increase organic (non-paid) traffic to the website by aligning its content, structure, and technical aspects with search engine algorithms and user expectations.

Key aspects of SEO include:

- Keyword research: Identifying relevant keywords and phrases that users may search for to find content related to the website.

- On-page optimization: Optimizing HTML elements (such as titles, headings, and meta descriptions) and content to align with target keywords and improve search engine visibility.
- Technical SEO: Ensuring the website's technical aspects, such as site speed, mobile-friendliness, and crawlability, are optimized for search engines.
- Link building: Earning or building high-quality backlinks from other reputable websites, which can improve the website's authority and visibility.
- User experience (UX): Providing a positive user experience through intuitive navigation, fast loading times, and engaging content to encourage users to stay on the website.

Interconnection between Website Accessibility and SEO:
While website accessibility and SEO are distinct areas, there are overlapping considerations. For example:

- Accessible websites tend to have well-structured content and clean HTML, which can positively impact SEO.
- Captions and transcripts provided for accessibility can also benefit SEO by making multimedia content more discoverable.
- Improved website usability resulting from accessibility practices can lead to better user engagement metrics, which can indirectly influence SEO rankings.

Both website accessibility and SEO contribute to a better user experience and broader inclusivity. By adopting inclusive design practices, providing accessible content, and optimizing for search engines, websites can enhance their visibility, reach, and overall impact.

7.5 Factors Affecting User Experience and SEO
User experience (UX) and SEO (Search Engine Optimization) are closely intertwined, as both aim to improve the performance, visibility, and satisfaction of website visitors. Several factors influence both user experience and SEO. Here are some key factors that affect both areas:

1. Website Speed:
Fast-loading websites enhance user experience by reducing waiting times and providing a seamless browsing experience. In terms of SEO, search engines prioritize fast-loading websites as they improve user satisfaction. Optimizing image sizes, minifying code, and utilizing caching techniques can improve website speed.

2. Mobile-Friendliness:
With the majority of internet users accessing websites on mobile devices, having a mobile-friendly website is crucial for both UX and SEO. Responsive design and ensuring that content is accessible and readable on different screen sizes contribute to positive user experiences and can improve search engine rankings.

3. Navigation and Information Architecture:
Intuitive and user-friendly website navigation positively impacts both UX and SEO. Clear navigation menus, logical hierarchy, and easy access to relevant content make it easier for users to find what they're looking for. Well-structured navigation also assists search engine crawlers in understanding and indexing website content.

4. Content Quality and Relevance:
High-quality, informative, and engaging content is vital for both UX and SEO. Users expect valuable and relevant information, while search engines prioritize content that satisfies user intent. Providing

well-written, comprehensive content that addresses user needs helps improve user experience and increases the likelihood of organic search visibility.

5. Readability and Accessibility:
Readable content that is easy to comprehend contributes to positive user experiences. Pay attention to font choices, font sizes, and line spacing to enhance readability. Additionally, ensuring accessibility for users with disabilities, such as providing alt text for images or captions for videos, improves both user experience and SEO.

6. Visual Design and Branding:
An appealing and consistent visual design creates a favourable user experience and supports brand recognition. Utilizing appropriate color schemes, typography, and imagery helps establish a visual identity. Consistent branding across the website enhances user trust and reinforces the website's credibility, positively impacting SEO.

7. Engagement and Interactivity:
Engaging users through interactive elements, such as forms, quizzes, or interactive media, improves user experience. Encouraging users to interact and spend more time on the website can improve engagement metrics, such as time on page or click-through rates, which can indirectly influence SEO rankings.

8. Accessibility of URLs and Site Structure:
Search engines and users appreciate websites with clean and accessible URLs and logical site structures. Descriptive URLs that reflect the content hierarchy and organized site structures make it easier for users to navigate and understand website content. Clear URL structures also assist search engines in indexing and ranking website pages effectively.

Optimizing these factors not only enhances user experience and satisfaction but also improves the overall search engine visibility and organic traffic to your website. By prioritizing both UX and SEO, you can create a website that meets user expectations while achieving your search engine optimization goals.

Chapter 8:
Monitoring and Analytics

8.1 Google Analytics Setup and Configuration
Setting up and configuring Google Analytics allows you to track and analyze user interactions and website performance, providing valuable insights for improving your website's effectiveness. Here's a step-by-step guide to set up Google Analytics for your website:

1. Sign Up for Google Analytics:
   - Go to the Google Analytics website (https://analytics.google.com/) and sign in with your Google account or create a new one.
   - Click on "Start for free" to begin the setup process.

2. Create a New Property:
   - Click on "Admin" in the bottom-left corner.
   - In the "Property" column, click on the dropdown menu and select "Create Property."
   - Choose "Web" as the property type.

3. Enter Property Details:
   - Enter the website name and website URL.
   - Select your reporting time zone and currency.

4. Get the Tracking ID:
   - Accept the Terms of Service agreement.
   - Click on "Create" to generate your Google Analytics tracking ID.

5. Implement the Tracking Code:
   - Once you have the tracking ID, copy the tracking code snippet provided by Google Analytics.
   - Paste the tracking code snippet into the `<head>` section of your website's HTML pages, just before the closing `</head>` tag.
   - Ensure that the tracking code is present on all pages of your website.

6. Verify Tracking:
   - After implementing the tracking code, go back to your Google Analytics account.
   - Click on "Home" in the left sidebar to access your Google Analytics dashboard.

- Google Analytics may take a few hours to start showing data. Once it's ready, you should see the "Real-time" data section showing active users on your website.

7. Configure Goals (Optional):
   - In Google Analytics, you can set up goals to track specific user actions, such as completing a form or making a purchase. This helps measure the effectiveness of your website's conversion funnel.
   - To set up goals, go to the "Admin" section, select the desired property, and click on "Goals." Follow the prompts to create your goals.

8. Enable E-commerce Tracking (If Applicable):
   - If your website has an e-commerce component, you can enable e-commerce tracking to track transactions, revenue, and other e-commerce-related metrics.
   - To enable e-commerce tracking, go to the "Admin" section, select the desired property, and click on "E-commerce Settings." Toggle the "Enable E-commerce" option.

9. Monitor and Analyze Data:
   - Once Google Analytics is set up, regularly access your Google Analytics dashboard to monitor key metrics, user behavior, traffic sources, and more.
   - Use the data to gain insights into your website's performance and make informed decisions for improvements.

Remember to keep the tracking code updated whenever you make changes to your website's structure or design. Regularly reviewing and analysing the data provided by Google Analytics will help you better understand your audience and optimize your website for better user experiences and results.

8.2 Tracking Key SEO Metrics and Performance
Tracking key SEO metrics and performance is essential to assess the effectiveness of your SEO efforts and make data-driven decisions to improve your website's search engine rankings. Here are the key SEO metrics you should track and how to monitor them:

1. Organic Traffic:
   - Track the total number of organic (non-paid) visits to your website over time.
   - Monitor changes in organic traffic to identify trends and measure the impact of SEO strategies.

2. Keyword Rankings:
   - Monitor the rankings of your target keywords in search engine results.
   - Use keyword tracking tools to track keyword positions and identify opportunities for improvement.

3. Click-Through Rate (CTR):
   - Measure the CTR of your website's pages in search results.
   - A high CTR indicates that your content is compelling and relevant to users.

4. Bounce Rate:
   - Track the percentage of visitors who leave your website after viewing only one page.
   - A high bounce rate may indicate that visitors aren't finding what they're looking for.

5. Page Load Time:
   - Monitor the time it takes for your web pages to load.
   - Faster-loading pages can improve user experience and SEO rankings.

6. Pages per Session:
   - Measure the average number of pages viewed per session.
   - Higher pages per session indicate better engagement with your content.

7. Conversion Rate:
   - Track the percentage of visitors who complete a desired action, such as making a purchase or filling out a form.
   - Monitoring conversion rates helps evaluate the effectiveness of your website's conversion funnel.

8. Backlinks and Referring Domains:
   - Monitor the number of backlinks and referring domains to your website.
   - High-quality backlinks from authoritative websites can positively impact SEO rankings.

9. Indexed Pages:
   - Ensure that search engines have indexed all relevant pages on your website.
   - Monitor the number of indexed pages to identify any indexing issues.

10. Mobile-Friendliness:
   - Ensure that your website is mobile-friendly and provides a positive user experience on mobile devices.
   - Use tools like Google's Mobile-Friendly Test to check your website's mobile-friendliness.

11. Crawling and Indexing Errors:
   - Regularly check for crawling and indexing errors in Google Search Console.
   - Address any crawl errors or indexing issues promptly to ensure optimal visibility.

12. Local SEO Metrics (If Applicable):
   - If you have a local business, track local SEO metrics such as local search rankings, Google My Business insights, and customer reviews.

Use tools like Google Analytics, Google Search Console, and other SEO analytics platforms to monitor these metrics. Regularly analyze the data and identify areas for improvement. A well-rounded SEO strategy considers both on-page optimization and off-page factors, aiming to provide a better user experience and increase organic search visibility.

8.3 Analysing Website Traffic and User Behavior
Analysing website traffic and user behavior is crucial to gaining insights into how visitors interact with your website. Understanding user behavior helps you identify strengths and weaknesses, make data-driven decisions, and optimize your website for better user experiences. Here's how to analyze website traffic and user behavior effectively:

1. Use Google Analytics:
   - Google Analytics is a powerful tool to analyze website traffic and user behavior. Install the tracking code on your website to start collecting data.
   - Access Google Analytics to view reports on user metrics, traffic sources, behavior flow, conversions, and more.

2. Review Key Metrics:
   - Focus on key metrics like total sessions, unique visitors, pageviews, and average session duration.

- Analyze trends over time to understand seasonal patterns and the impact of marketing campaigns or website changes.

3. Understand Traffic Sources:
   - Identify the sources of your website traffic, including organic search, direct, referral, social media, and paid advertising.
   - Evaluate which sources drive the most traffic and conversions to optimize your marketing efforts.

4. Analyze Page Performance:
   - Identify high-traffic pages, popular content, and pages with high bounce rates or low average time on page.
   - Optimize low-performing pages to improve engagement and user experience.

5. Examine User Behavior Flow:
   - Use behavior flow reports to visualize how users navigate through your website.
   - Identify common paths, drop-off points, and opportunities for improving the user journey.

6. Monitor Conversion Funnels:
   - Set up goals and conversion funnels to track user actions leading to specific outcomes (e.g., form submissions or purchases).
   - Analyze funnel drop-offs to identify where users abandon the conversion process.

7. Conduct A/B Testing:
   - Implement A/B tests to compare different versions of pages and elements (e.g., headlines, CTAs, layouts).
   - Use A/B testing results to optimize website elements for better performance.

8. Utilize Heatmaps:
   - Use heatmaps to visualize user interaction patterns, clicks, and scrolling behavior on web pages.
   - Heatmaps provide valuable insights into areas of interest and potential usability issues.

9. Monitor Exit Pages:
   - Identify pages with high exit rates to understand why users are leaving your website.
   - Optimize these pages to encourage further exploration or conversions.

10. Analyze Demographics and Behavior:
   - Use Google Analytics demographic reports to understand the age, gender, location, and interests of your audience.
   - Tailor your content and marketing strategies based on audience insights.

11. Set Up Custom Reports:
   - Create custom reports in Google Analytics to focus on specific metrics or segments relevant to your business goals.
   - Custom reports allow you to dive deeper into data tailored to your needs.

Regularly analyze the data and use the insights gained to optimize your website for improved user experiences and better performance. By understanding user behavior, you can make informed decisions that lead to increased engagement, conversions, and overall success of your website.

8.4 SEO Audit and Reporting

Conducting an SEO audit and generating regular SEO reports are essential practices to assess the health and performance of your website in search engine rankings. An SEO audit helps identify areas that need improvement, while SEO reports provide stakeholders with valuable insights and progress updates. Here's how to perform an SEO audit and create SEO reports:

1. SEO Audit:
  - Evaluate On-Page SEO:
    - Review meta titles, meta descriptions, and heading tags for keyword optimization and relevance.
    - Check for keyword usage in content and ensure it aligns with user intent.
    - Analyze URL structure and ensure it is descriptive and user-friendly.

  - Assess Technical SEO:
    - Check for proper website indexing in search engines.
    - Review XML sitemaps and robots.txt files for correct setup.
    - Ensure the website is mobile-friendly and has fast page load times.
    - Check for broken links, crawl errors, and duplicate content.

  - Analyze Backlinks and Off-Page SEO:
    - Review the backlink profile for quality and relevancy.
    - Identify and disavow spammy or harmful backlinks.
    - Assess the website's presence on social media and other online platforms.

  - Conduct Keyword Research and Competitor Analysis:
    - Identify relevant target keywords and search terms for your industry.
    - Analyze competitors' SEO strategies and rankings to identify opportunities.

  - User Experience and Content Audit:
    - Evaluate website usability, navigation, and overall user experience.
    - Review content quality, relevancy, and engagement metrics.
    - Check for opportunities to improve content and user engagement.

  - Local SEO (if applicable):
    - Optimize Google My Business listing and local citations.
    - Ensure NAP (Name, Address, Phone Number) consistency across the web.

2. SEO Reporting:
  - Set Clear Goals: Define specific SEO objectives and key performance indicators (KPIs) for your reporting.
  - Choose the Right Metrics: Select metrics that align with your goals, such as organic traffic, keyword rankings, backlinks, and conversion rates.
  - Use Google Analytics: Utilize Google Analytics to track and measure website traffic and user behavior.
  - Use SEO Tools: Use SEO tools like Google Search Console, Ahrefs, SEMrush, or Moz to gather data and insights.
  - Create Custom Reports: Generate custom reports tailored to your stakeholders' needs and interests.
  - Provide Actionable Insights: Offer actionable recommendations based on the data, highlighting areas for improvement and growth.
  - Regular Reporting: Create periodic reports (e.g., monthly or quarterly) to track progress over time and measure the impact of SEO efforts.

By conducting regular SEO audits and generating comprehensive SEO reports, you can identify areas of improvement, track the success of your SEO strategies, and demonstrate the value of your efforts to stakeholders. Continuous monitoring and optimization based on the audit findings and reports are essential for maintaining a competitive edge in search engine rankings.

8.5 Staying Updated with Algorithm Changes

Staying updated with algorithm changes is crucial for any SEO practitioner or website owner. Search engines, especially Google, frequently update their algorithms to deliver more relevant and accurate search results to users. Here are some strategies to stay informed about algorithm changes:

1. Follow Official Announcements:
   - Keep an eye on official announcements and updates from search engine companies like Google, Bing, and others. They often release official statements or blog posts about significant algorithm changes.

2. Subscribe to Webmaster Communication Channels:
   - Sign up for Google Webmaster Central and Bing Webmaster Tools to receive email notifications about updates, best practices, and announcements.

3. Monitor SEO News and Blogs:
   - Follow reputable SEO news websites, blogs, and forums that regularly cover search engine algorithm updates and industry news.
   - Some popular SEO news sources include Search Engine Land, Search Engine Journal, Moz Blog, and SEMrush Blog.

4. Follow SEO Experts on Social Media:
   - Connect with reputable SEO experts and influencers on platforms like Twitter and LinkedIn.
   - They often share insights and updates related to search engine algorithms.

5. Attend SEO Conferences and Webinars:
   - Participate in SEO conferences, webinars, and virtual events where industry experts discuss the latest trends and algorithm changes.
   - Networking with other SEO professionals can also provide valuable insights.

6. Join SEO Community Groups:
   - Join SEO community groups on platforms like Facebook, Reddit, or LinkedIn to discuss algorithm changes and industry trends.
   - These groups can be a valuable source of real-time information and discussions.

7. Read Google's Webmaster Guidelines:
   - Familiarize yourself with Google's Webmaster Guidelines, which provide insights into the best practices recommended by Google.

8. Monitor Search Engine Results Pages (SERPs):
   - Regularly monitor the search engine results pages (SERPs) for your target keywords to observe any significant changes.

9. Analyze Website Traffic and Rankings:
   - Monitor your website's organic traffic and keyword rankings regularly.
   - Sudden drops in traffic or rankings may indicate algorithm changes affecting your site.

10. Test and Adapt:
   - Conduct experiments and tests to understand how algorithm changes impact your website's performance.
   - Be prepared to adapt your SEO strategies based on the results of these tests.

Remember that algorithm updates are a regular part of the SEO landscape. Staying informed and adapting your strategies accordingly will help you maintain a competitive edge and ensure your website's visibility in search engine results.

Chapter 9:
Local SEO Strategies

9.1 Importance of Local SEO
Local SEO is of paramount importance for businesses with a physical presence or those targeting a specific local audience. It focuses on optimizing a website to appear in local search results when users search for products or services in a specific geographic area. Here are the key reasons why local SEO is crucial:

1. Increased Online Visibility:
   Local SEO helps businesses appear in local search results and on Google Maps, making it easier for potential customers to find them when searching for relevant products or services nearby.

2. Targeted Local Traffic:
   Local SEO drives targeted traffic from users in the vicinity who are more likely to convert into customers. These users are actively looking for local businesses to fulfil their immediate needs.

3. Mobile Search and "Near Me" Searches:
   With the rise of mobile usage, "near me" searches have become increasingly popular. Local SEO ensures businesses show up for these location-based searches, increasing the chances of attracting nearby customers.

4. Improved Google My Business (GMB) Presence:
   Optimizing Google My Business listing with accurate NAP (Name, Address, Phone Number), business hours, reviews, and photos enhances a business's local online presence and credibility.

5. Positive Reviews and Reputation:
   Local SEO encourages businesses to solicit and respond to customer reviews. Positive reviews build trust and attract more customers, while addressing negative reviews demonstrates responsiveness and customer care.

6. Cost-Effectiveness:

Local SEO is relatively cost-effective compared to traditional advertising methods. It targets users actively seeking local businesses, leading to higher conversion rates and a better return on investment (ROI).

7. Beat Local Competitors:
Implementing effective local SEO strategies helps businesses stand out from local competitors. It can level the playing field for smaller businesses competing with larger corporations.

8. Voice Search Optimization:
With the growing popularity of voice search, local SEO becomes even more critical. Voice search queries often have a local intent, and businesses optimized for local SEO have an advantage in voice search results.

9. Local Pack and Featured Snippets:
Local SEO increases the chances of appearing in the local pack (the top 3 business listings) and featured snippets for local searches, improving brand visibility.

10. In-Store Foot Traffic:
For brick-and-mortar businesses, local SEO can drive more in-store foot traffic by providing essential information like directions and store hours to potential customers.

Overall, local SEO helps businesses connect with their target audience, boost online visibility, and drive valuable traffic to their physical locations or websites. It is an indispensable marketing strategy for any business with a local focus and an essential component of an effective digital marketing plan.

9.2 Optimizing Google My Business Profile
Optimizing your Google My Business (GMB) profile is crucial for improving your local online presence and increasing visibility in local search results. A well-optimized GMB profile enhances your chances of appearing in the local pack and Google Maps, attracting potential customers looking for products or services in your area. Here are the key steps to optimize your GMB profile:

1. Claim and Verify Your Business:
  - Sign in to your Google account and claim your business listing on Google My Business.
  - Verify your ownership through a postcard, phone call, email, or instant verification (available for some businesses).

2. Complete Your Business Information:
  - Provide accurate and consistent information, including business name, address, phone number (NAP), website URL, and business hours.
  - Use your official business name and avoid keyword stuffing.

3. Choose Relevant Categories:
  - Select the primary and secondary categories that best describe your business. Be specific and use categories that match your products or services.

4. Write a Compelling Business Description:
  - Craft a concise and engaging business description (up to 750 characters) that highlights your unique selling points and what sets you apart from competitors.

5. Add High-Quality Photos:

- Upload high-resolution photos of your business, products, services, team, and interior. Include a profile photo (e.g., your logo) and a cover photo that represents your business.

6. Gather and Respond to Reviews:
   - Encourage customers to leave reviews on your GMB listing. Respond to both positive and negative reviews promptly and professionally to demonstrate your customer service.

7. Display Accurate Business Hours:
   - Keep your business hours updated, including special hours for holidays or events.

8. Enable Messaging:
   - Allow customers to message you directly through the GMB listing. Respond to messages promptly to engage with potential customers.

9. Add Services or Products:
   - If applicable, list specific services or products you offer. This helps customers understand what your business provides.

10. Geo-Tag Photos:
   - Geo-tag your photos with the specific locations where they were taken. This can help enhance your local relevance.

11. Utilize Google Posts:
   - Use Google Posts to share updates, promotions, events, and offers directly on your GMB listing. Posts appear in search results and can attract attention.

12. Monitor Insights:
   - Regularly review the insights and analytics provided by GMB to understand how customers find your business and what actions they take.

13. Address Q&A:
   - Monitor and answer customer questions in the Q&A section to provide helpful information and address inquiries.

By following these steps, you can optimize your Google My Business profile for better visibility in local search results and improve your chances of attracting local customers to your business. A well-optimized GMB profile enhances your local SEO efforts and contributes to a positive online reputation.

9.3 Local Keyword Research and Targeting
Local keyword research and targeting are essential for businesses aiming to attract local customers and improve their visibility in local search results. By understanding the specific search terms used by local users, businesses can optimize their content, website, and Google My Business listing for better local SEO. Here's how to perform local keyword research and effectively target local keywords:

1. Identify Local Search Intent:
   - Understand the intent behind local searches. Users often include location-specific terms (e.g., city, neighbourhood, "near me") when searching for local products or services.

2. Use Keyword Research Tools:

  - Utilize keyword research tools like Google Keyword Planner, Ahrefs, SEMrush, or Uber suggest to find relevant local keywords.
  - Focus on keywords with local intent, such as "best restaurants in [city]," "hair salons near me," or "plumbers in [neighbourhood]."

3. Analyze Competitors:
  - Analyze the websites and Google My Business listings of local competitors.
  - Identify the keywords they are targeting and how they optimize their content for local searches.

4. Long-Tail Keywords:
  - Target long-tail keywords that include specific local modifiers (e.g., "cheap hotels in [city]," "24-hour pizza delivery in [neighbourhood]").
  - Long-tail keywords are more specific and often have lower competition, increasing your chances of ranking higher.

5. Google Autocomplete and Related Searches:
  - Use Google Autocomplete suggestions to find popular local search queries related to your business.
  - Scroll to the bottom of Google search results to view "Searches related to [your query]" for more keyword ideas.

6. Location-Specific Landing Pages:
  - Create location-specific landing pages on your website, each optimized for a particular local keyword or area.
  - Include the location name in the page title, meta description, heading tags, and content.

7. Optimize Google My Business (GMB) Listing:
  - Incorporate local keywords into your GMB business description, products/services, and Google Posts.
  - Use location-specific keywords in GMB attributes like service area or service radius.

8. Local Citations and Directories:
  - Include your business name, address, phone number, and website URL (NAP+W) in local citations and directories.
  - Consistent NAP+W data across the web improves local SEO.

9. Monitor and Adjust:
  - Regularly monitor your local keyword rankings and website traffic through Google Analytics and other SEO tools.
  - Analyze performance and make adjustments to your local keyword targeting as needed.

10. User Experience:
  - Prioritize user experience on your website and landing pages.
  - Make it easy for local users to find relevant information and take action.

By conducting local keyword research and targeting, businesses can align their content and web presence with the search terms used by their local audience. This enhances their local SEO strategy and improves the chances of reaching and attracting potential customers within their target area.

9.4 Local Citations and Online Reviews
Local citations and online reviews play a significant role in local SEO and can have a substantial impact on a business's online reputation and visibility in local search results. Understanding and managing these aspects are crucial for businesses looking to attract local customers and build trust within their communities. Here's a breakdown of local citations and online reviews:

1. Local Citations:
   - Local citations refer to online mentions of a business's name, address, phone number, and website (NAP+W) across various websites, directories, and platforms.
   - Consistent and accurate NAP+W information is essential for local SEO as it signals to search engines that your business is legitimate and helps establish its location and relevance.

2. Types of Local Citations:
   - Structured Citations: These are mentions of your business in online directories, local business listings, and social media profiles.
   - Unstructured Citations: These are mentions of your business on blogs, news articles, and other websites without a specific directory-like format.

3. Importance of Local Citations:
   - Local SEO Signal: Consistent NAP+W data across different platforms validates your business's legitimacy and location to search engines.
   - Increased Online Visibility: Citations in various local directories can lead to higher visibility in local search results.
   - Improved Local Rankings: Quality citations can positively impact your business's local search rankings.
   - Local Business Trust: Having accurate and consistent NAP+W information builds trust with potential customers.

4. Managing Local Citations:
   - Ensure Consistency: Verify that your business's NAP+W information is consistent across all online directories, social media platforms, and websites.
   - Correct Inaccuracies: Regularly monitor and correct any discrepancies or outdated information in your citations.
   - Audit Your Citations: Conduct periodic audits to ensure that your business is listed accurately and completely on relevant platforms.

5. Online Reviews:
   - Online reviews are customer feedback and opinions about your business posted on review sites like Google My Business, Yelp, Facebook, and other platforms.
   - Positive reviews build trust and credibility, while negative reviews can impact your reputation if not addressed properly.

6. Importance of Online Reviews:
   - Influence Customer Decisions: Potential customers often rely on online reviews to make informed decisions about products or services.
   - Local Search Rankings: Positive reviews can positively influence local search rankings, while the quantity and sentiment of reviews are ranking factors.

7. Managing Online Reviews:

- Encourage Reviews: Ask satisfied customers to leave reviews, but avoid offering incentives or paying for reviews.
  - Respond to Reviews: Respond to all reviews, positive or negative, in a professional and courteous manner. Address concerns and show appreciation for positive feedback.
  - Monitor Reviews: Regularly monitor and track reviews across platforms to address issues promptly and engage with customers.

Managing local citations and online reviews is an ongoing process that requires proactive monitoring and engagement. By maintaining consistent NAP+W data and cultivating positive customer feedback, businesses can enhance their local online presence, build trust with customers, and improve their local SEO performance.

9.5 Local Link Building and Outreach

Local link building and outreach are crucial strategies for improving a business's local SEO and online visibility within its community. Building relevant, high-quality local backlinks can boost a business's authority and credibility, leading to higher search engine rankings. Here's how to effectively perform local link building and outreach:

1. Identify Local Link Opportunities:
  - Look for local businesses, organizations, and community websites that may be interested in linking to your business.
  - Seek out local event sponsorships, partnerships, and collaborations that can lead to link opportunities.

2. Create Valuable Local Content:
  - Develop valuable and shareable content that appeals to the local community, such as local guides, event coverage, or informative articles about local topics.

3. Local Business Directories and Chambers of Commerce:
  - List your business on reputable local business directories, chambers of commerce websites, and community platforms.
  - Many of these platforms allow you to include a link back to your website.

4. Local News and Media Coverage:
  - Engage with local journalists and reporters to share newsworthy stories about your business, events, or community involvement.
  - Media coverage can lead to valuable local backlinks.

5. Sponsor Local Events or Charities:
  - Sponsor local events, fundraisers, or charities, and ask for a link on their websites as a sponsor acknowledgment.

6. Guest Blogging:
  - Offer to write guest blog posts for local blogs or publications. In exchange, you can include a link back to your website in the author bio.

7. Partner with Local Influencers:
  - Collaborate with local influencers or bloggers in your niche to promote your products, services, or events.

- Influencers may link back to your website or share your content with their audience.

8. Host Local Events or Workshops:
   - Organize and host local events or workshops that align with your business. Promote these events to attract attendees and potential backlinks from event listings.

9. Engage with Local Community Online:
   - Participate in local community forums, social media groups, and discussion platforms.
   - Engaging in conversations and providing helpful insights can lead to link opportunities.

10. Outreach and Relationship Building:
   - Reach out to local businesses, organizations, and influencers with personalized emails or messages, explaining the mutual benefits of linking to each other.

11. Monitor Competitors' Backlinks:
   - Use SEO tools to monitor the backlink profiles of local competitors and identify potential link opportunities they have acquired.

Remember, the key to successful local link building is to focus on quality over quantity. Aim for relevant, authoritative, and locally-focused backlinks that can genuinely benefit your website and improve your local search rankings. Building strong relationships within the local community and engaging in meaningful outreach efforts can lead to more opportunities for valuable local backlinks.

Chapter 10:
E-Commerce SEO

10.1 SEO Strategies for E-Commerce Websites
SEO strategies are crucial for the success of e-commerce websites as they can significantly impact their online visibility, organic traffic, and sales. Here are some essential SEO strategies specifically tailored for e-commerce websites:

1. Keyword Research:
  - Conduct extensive keyword research to identify relevant and high-intent keywords related to your products.
  - Use keyword research tools and consider long-tail keywords to target specific user search queries.

2. Optimized Product Pages:
  - Optimize product pages with unique and descriptive titles, meta descriptions, and heading tags.
  - Include high-quality images, detailed product descriptions, and customer reviews to enhance user experience and provide valuable information.

3. User-Friendly URLs:
  - Use clean and SEO-friendly URLs that include relevant keywords and product names instead of long strings of numbers or symbols.

4. Mobile Optimization:
  - Ensure your e-commerce website is mobile-friendly and offers a seamless experience for users on smartphones and tablets.
  - Mobile optimization is crucial for both user experience and search engine rankings.

5. Site Speed and Performance:
  - Improve site speed and performance to reduce bounce rates and improve user satisfaction.
  - Compress images, leverage browser caching, and consider using a Content Delivery Network (CDN).

6. Implement Rich Snippets and Schema Markup:

- Utilize structured data markup (Schema.org) to provide search engines with additional context about your products, prices, reviews, and availability.
   - Rich snippets can enhance your search results appearance and attract more clicks.

7. Internal Linking:
   - Implement a strategic internal linking structure to connect related products and categories.
   - Internal linking helps search engines understand the structure of your website and improves user navigation.

8. Optimize Category Pages:
   - Apply SEO best practices to category pages, including relevant titles, descriptions, and engaging content.
   - Use category pages as landing pages for targeted keywords.

9. Focus on Customer Reviews:
   - Encourage customers to leave reviews for products, as they can improve your website's trustworthiness and influence purchasing decisions.

10. Implement Secure Sockets Layer (SSL) Certificate:
   - Install an SSL certificate to ensure that your website is secure and that customer data is protected during transactions.

11. Create Informative Content:
   - Develop a blog or resource section to publish informative content related to your products, industry, and customer needs.
   - Informative content can attract organic traffic and establish your e-commerce brand as an authority in the field.

12. Optimize for Local SEO (if applicable):
   - If your e-commerce business has physical locations or serves specific regions, optimize for local SEO with local keywords, Google My Business listing, and local citations.

13. Monitor and Analyze Performance:
   - Regularly monitor SEO performance using analytics tools such as Google Analytics and Google Search Console.
   - Analyze data to identify areas for improvement and adjust your strategies accordingly.

Remember, SEO for e-commerce is an ongoing process that requires continuous monitoring, testing, and optimization. By implementing these strategies, you can improve your e-commerce website's visibility in search engine results and attract more qualified traffic, ultimately leading to increased sales and revenue.

10.2 Product Page Optimization
Product page optimization is essential for e-commerce websites to attract potential customers, improve user experience, and increase conversions. A well-optimized product page provides valuable information, engages users, and encourages them to make a purchase. Here are some key strategies for optimizing product pages:

1. Compelling Product Titles:
   - Use descriptive and engaging product titles that include relevant keywords.
   - Highlight the main benefit or unique selling point of the product.

2. High-Quality Product Images:
  - Include multiple high-resolution images that showcase the product from different angles.
  - Use zoom functionality to allow users to inspect product details.

3. Clear and Informative Product Descriptions:
  - Write clear, concise, and informative product descriptions that accurately describe the product's features, benefits, and specifications.
  - Use bullet points to make key details easy to scan.

4. Implement User Reviews and Ratings:
  - Display customer reviews and ratings to build trust and credibility.
  - Positive reviews can influence purchasing decisions.

5. Prominent Call-to-Action (CTA):
  - Place a clear and prominent CTA button that encourages users to add the product to their cart or make a purchase.
  - Use action-oriented words like "Buy Now," "Add to Cart," or "Shop Now."

6. Price and Shipping Information:
  - Display the product price prominently and clearly.
  - Provide transparent shipping information, including shipping costs and delivery times.

7. Stock Availability:
  - Indicate the product's stock availability, especially if it's limited or low in stock.
  - Use urgency messages like "Only 2 left in stock" to create a sense of scarcity.

8. Trust Symbols and Security:
  - Display trust symbols, security badges, and SSL certificates to assure customers that their transactions are secure.
  - Highlight any security measures in place to protect customer data.

9. Cross-Selling and Related Products:
  - Include sections for related products or complementary items to encourage cross-selling.
  - Use "Customers who bought this also bought" or "You may also like" suggestions.

10. Mobile-Friendly Design:
  - Ensure that product pages are optimized for mobile devices with easy navigation and readable content.
  - Mobile users should be able to view product images and information without any issues.

11. Fast Page Load Speed:
  - Optimize images and use caching to improve page load speed.
  - A fast-loading product page reduces bounce rates and improves user experience.

12. Schema Markup for Rich Snippets:
  - Implement structured data (Schema.org) to enhance product pages with rich snippets in search results.
  - Rich snippets can display additional product details like price, availability, and reviews.

13. A/B Testing:

- Conduct A/B testing to experiment with different page elements, layouts, and CTAs to determine the most effective combination for conversions.

By applying these product page optimization strategies, e-commerce websites can create an enticing and user-friendly shopping experience, which ultimately leads to increased sales and customer satisfaction. Continuous monitoring and improvement of product pages based on user feedback and analytics data can further enhance the performance and effectiveness of product pages.

10.3 Category and Navigation Structure
A well-organized category and navigation structure is crucial for e-commerce websites to provide a seamless and user-friendly browsing experience. A clear and intuitive structure helps visitors find products quickly, encourages them to explore more, and ultimately boosts conversions. Here are some strategies to optimize the category and navigation structure:

1. Logical Category Hierarchy:
  - Create a logical and hierarchical category structure that reflects the organization of your products.
  - Each category should have subcategories as needed, creating a tree-like navigation.

2. Clear and Descriptive Labels:
  - Use clear and descriptive labels for categories and subcategories, using familiar terms that customers understand.
  - Avoid jargon or confusing terminology.

3. Limit the Number of Categories:
  - Keep the number of top-level categories manageable to avoid overwhelming users.
  - Use subcategories to further refine products within broader categories.

4. Mega Menus or Dropdowns:
  - Consider using mega menus or dropdowns to display subcategories and featured products.
  - Mega menus can provide a quick overview of product offerings and aid navigation.

5. Use Breadcrumbs:
  - Implement breadcrumbs at the top of each page to show users their current location within the category structure.
  - Breadcrumbs help users navigate back to previous pages easily.

6. Search Functionality:
  - Include a prominent search bar to allow users to quickly find specific products or categories.
  - Implement autocomplete and typo tolerance to enhance the search experience.

7. Filter and Sorting Options:
  - Offer filter and sorting options on category pages to help users narrow down their product search based on attributes like price, brand, size, color, etc.

8. Use Visual Cues:
  - Use visual cues like icons or images to represent categories and subcategories.
  - Visual cues help users quickly identify the type of products within each category.

9. Showcase Featured and New Products:
  - Use the category pages to showcase featured or new products related to each category.

- Feature products with high demand or promotions to attract attention.

10. User Testing and Feedback:
   - Conduct user testing to evaluate the category and navigation structure's usability and effectiveness.
   - Gather feedback from users to identify pain points and areas for improvement.

11. Responsive Design:
   - Ensure that the category and navigation structure is fully responsive, providing a seamless experience across all devices, including mobile and tablets.

12. Monitor Analytics Data:
   - Regularly monitor user behavior and engagement using analytics tools.
   - Analyze data on category page performance, bounce rates, and conversion rates to identify areas for optimization.

A well-optimized category and navigation structure can significantly improve user experience, increase the time users spend on your website, and lead to higher conversion rates. Continuously review and optimize the structure based on user feedback and data to ensure it meets the changing needs of your customers and aligns with your business goals.

10.4 User Reviews and Ratings
User reviews and ratings are powerful tools for e-commerce websites to build trust, credibility, and transparency with potential customers. Positive reviews and high ratings can significantly influence purchasing decisions, while negative reviews present opportunities for improvement. Here are some strategies to leverage user reviews and ratings effectively:

1. Encourage Reviews:
   - Promptly request reviews from customers after they make a purchase.
   - Use email follow-ups or post-purchase pop-ups to request feedback.

2. Provide Multiple Review Options:
   - Offer various review platforms, such as on-site reviews, Google Reviews, Trustpilot, or industry-specific review sites.
   - Diversifying platforms can encourage customers to leave reviews on their preferred sites.

3. Make Reviewing Easy:
   - Simplify the review process by providing a clear and user-friendly interface.
   - Avoid requiring customers to create accounts to leave a review.

4. Respond to Reviews:
   - Respond to all reviews, both positive and negative, in a professional and courteous manner.
   - Address concerns raised in negative reviews and thank customers for positive feedback.

5. Showcase Reviews:
   - Display customer reviews prominently on product pages to build trust with potential buyers.
   - Use review snippets or testimonials on the homepage or landing pages.

6. Use Schema Markup:

- Implement schema markup to add review stars to search engine results, making your website more appealing to users.

7. Incentivize Reviews:
   - Offer incentives like discounts or loyalty points to customers who leave reviews.
   - However, avoid directly incentivizing positive reviews to maintain authenticity.

8. Moderate Reviews:
   - Monitor and moderate reviews to ensure they adhere to community guidelines.
   - Remove spam or inappropriate content while allowing genuine customer feedback.

9. Address Negative Reviews:
   - Respond to negative reviews constructively and offer solutions to address customer concerns.
   - Use negative reviews as opportunities for improvement and customer service enhancement.

10. Highlight User-Generated Content:
   - Share user-generated content, such as photos or videos of customers using your products, on social media or product pages.
   - User-generated content enhances authenticity and builds brand trust.

11. Use Reviews in Marketing:
   - Incorporate positive reviews in marketing materials, email campaigns, or advertisements.
   - Highlighting real customer experiences can influence potential buyers positively.

12. Analyze and Learn:
   - Analyze review trends and feedback to identify areas for improvement in products or services.
   - Use insights from reviews to make data-driven business decisions.

Positive reviews and high ratings can serve as social proof, convincing potential customers to trust your brand and make a purchase. Embrace user reviews as an integral part of your e-commerce strategy and engage with your customers to foster a strong and loyal customer base.

10.5 SEO for E-Commerce Platforms
SEO for e-commerce platforms is a specialized area that involves optimizing online stores to improve their organic visibility in search engine results. As e-commerce websites often have numerous product pages and unique challenges, specific SEO strategies are essential to attract more organic traffic and drive sales. Here are some key SEO practices for e-commerce platforms:

1. Keyword Research for Products:
   - Perform keyword research to identify relevant and high-converting keywords for each product.
   - Target long-tail keywords and specific product attributes to reach the right audience.

2. Unique Product Descriptions:
   - Avoid using manufacturer-provided product descriptions. Write unique, informative, and SEO-friendly descriptions for each product.
   - Use relevant keywords naturally within the descriptions.

3. Optimized Product Titles and Meta Tags:
   - Create compelling product titles with relevant keywords and features.

- Write unique meta titles and meta descriptions for each product page, incorporating relevant keywords.

4. User-Friendly URLs:
   - Use user-friendly and SEO-friendly URLs that include relevant keywords and product names.
   - Avoid using dynamic URLs with special characters or excessive parameters.

5. Image Optimization:
   - Optimize product images by using descriptive alt tags and appropriate file names.
   - Compress images to improve site loading speed.

6. Site Structure and Navigation:
   - Ensure a logical and user-friendly site structure with easy navigation.
   - Implement breadcrumb navigation to aid users and search engines in understanding page hierarchy.

7. Internal Linking:
   - Utilize internal linking to connect related products and categories.
   - Improve link flow within your website to distribute link equity.

8. User Reviews and Ratings:
   - Enable user reviews and ratings for products to build trust and improve click-through rates.
   - Rich snippets and review stars can be included in search results using schema markup.

9. Mobile Optimization:
   - Optimize your e-commerce site for mobile devices, ensuring a smooth user experience.
   - Google prioritizes mobile-friendly sites in its search rankings.

10. Page Loading Speed:
   - Optimize page loading speed to reduce bounce rates and improve user experience.
   - Use tools like Google PageSpeed Insights to identify and fix performance issues.

11. Secure Checkout Process:
   - Ensure a secure and straightforward checkout process to build customer trust.
   - Use SSL certificates to encrypt customer data during transactions.

12. XML Sitemap:
   - Create and submit an XML sitemap to search engines to help them crawl and index your product pages more efficiently.

13. Monitoring and Analytics:
   - Monitor website traffic, search rankings, and user behavior using tools like Google Analytics and Google Search Console.
   - Analyze data to identify opportunities for improvement and track the effectiveness of SEO efforts.

By implementing these SEO strategies, e-commerce platforms can enhance their online presence, attract relevant organic traffic, and ultimately increase conversions and sales. Remember that SEO for e-commerce is an ongoing process, and continuous monitoring and optimization are necessary to stay competitive in the ever-evolving digital landscape.

Chapter 11:
International SEO

11.1 Expanding Your Website's Reach to International Markets

Expanding your website's reach to international markets is an exciting opportunity to tap into a global audience and grow your business beyond borders. However, it requires careful planning, localization, and SEO strategies to effectively target international users. Here are some steps to expand your website's reach to international markets:

1. Market Research:
   - Conduct thorough market research to identify potential international markets with demand for your products or services.
   - Analyze competition, local preferences, and cultural differences.

2. Choose Target Countries:
   - Select target countries based on market research, language similarities, shipping feasibility, and legal considerations.
   - Start with a few countries initially to focus your efforts effectively.

3. Website Localization:
   - Localize your website content, including product descriptions, landing pages, and user interface, to the languages of your target countries.
   - Use professional translators to ensure accurate translations and cultural context.

4. International SEO:
   - Implement international SEO best practices, including hreflang tags, to signal to search engines the language and country targeting of your pages.

  - Use country-specific domains (ccTLDs), subdomains, or subdirectories to differentiate your international content.

5. Currency and Payment Options:
  - Offer multiple currency options and payment gateways to accommodate international customers' preferences.
  - Display prices in local currencies for a seamless shopping experience.

6. Shipping and Fulfilment:
  - Plan efficient shipping and fulfilment methods for international orders.
  - Consider partnering with international logistics providers to streamline the process.

7. Customer Support:
  - Provide multilingual customer support to assist international customers.
  - Offer support through various channels, such as email, live chat, or social media.

8. International Legal and Regulatory Compliance:
  - Understand and comply with international laws and regulations related to e-commerce, taxation, and data privacy in each target country.

9. Monitor Local Trends and Preferences:
  - Stay up-to-date with local trends and preferences in your target markets.
  - Adapt your products, marketing strategies, and promotions accordingly.

10. Partner with Local Influencers:
  - Collaborate with local influencers or bloggers to promote your brand in the target countries.
  - Influencers can help you reach a wider audience and establish credibility.

11. Use Social Media Platforms:
  - Utilize social media platforms popular in your target countries to engage with local audiences and promote your products.

12. Measure and Adjust:
  - Use web analytics tools to measure the performance of your international efforts.
  - Analyze data to identify areas for improvement and adjust your strategies accordingly.

Expanding to international markets requires a thoughtful approach and ongoing commitment to understanding and meeting the needs of diverse audiences. With the right strategies and localization efforts, you can successfully expand your website's reach and tap into new markets around the world.

11.2 Language and Country Targeting
Language and country targeting are essential aspects of international SEO that help search engines understand which audience each page of your website is intended for. Properly implementing language and country targeting signals can improve the relevance of your content for specific regions and languages, leading to better search rankings and user experience. Here's how to effectively implement language and country targeting:

1. Hreflang Tags:
  - Use hreflang tags to specify the language and geographic targeting of each page on your website.

- Hreflang tags inform search engines about the intended audience for each page, helping them deliver the correct version to users.

2. Language Targeting:
  - Create versions of your website in different languages to cater to users who speak those languages.
  - Use separate URLs or subdirectories for each language version (e.g., example.com/en/ for English and example.com/es/ for Spanish).

3. Country Targeting:
  - If your website targets specific countries, use country-specific domain extensions (ccTLDs) like .uk, .fr, .de, etc.
  - Alternatively, use subdomains (e.g., uk.example.com) or subdirectories (e.g., example.com/uk/) for country-specific content.

4. Content Localization:
  - Localize the content on your website for each targeted country or language.
  - Translate and adapt product descriptions, landing pages, and other content to suit the cultural preferences of each region.

5. Webmaster Tools:
  - Register your international versions of the website with Google Search Console or other webmaster tools.
  - Use the geotargeting feature to specify the target country for each version.

6. Language Selector:
  - Provide a clear language selector or dropdown menu on your website to allow users to switch between language versions easily.

7. Geo-IP Redirection:
  - Use geo-IP redirection to automatically redirect users to the appropriate language or country version of your website based on their location.

8. Localized Meta Tags:
  - Optimize meta titles and descriptions for each language and country version of your pages.
  - Use relevant keywords in the local language to improve search engine visibility.

9. Avoid Duplicate Content:
  - Ensure that each page is properly targeted and has unique content to avoid duplicate content issues.
  - Canonicalize similar pages if necessary to indicate the preferred version.

10. Language and Country Switching:
  - Allow users to switch between language and country versions easily without disrupting their browsing experience.
  - Avoid automatic redirection without user consent.

11. Test and Monitor:
  - Test the implementation of language and country targeting thoroughly to ensure it works as intended.

- Monitor website traffic and search rankings to identify any issues and make adjustments as needed.

By effectively implementing language and country targeting, you can provide a more relevant and personalized experience to international users, increase your website's visibility in global search results, and attract a broader audience from diverse regions and language groups.

11.3 Href lang Tags and International URLs
Hreflang tags and international URLs are crucial elements in international SEO that help search engines understand the language and geographical targeting of your website's pages. Properly implementing hreflang tags and international URLs ensures that search engines deliver the right version of your content to users in specific regions and languages. Here's a detailed explanation of each:

1. Hreflang Tags:
   - Hreflang tags are HTML tags that specify the language and/or regional targeting of a web page. They are placed in the head section of a page's HTML code.
   - Hreflang tags help search engines understand which language version of a page to show in search results based on the user's language preference or geographical location.

2. How Hreflang Tags Work:
   - For Language Targeting: Use the "rel" attribute with a value of "alternate" and specify the language code (e.g., "en" for English) and the URL of the equivalent page in that language.
   - For Country or Region Targeting: Use the "rel" attribute with a value of "alternate" and include the language code and the country or region code (e.g., "en-GB" for English in the United Kingdom) along with the URL of the equivalent page for that region.

3. Example of Hreflang Tags for Language Targeting:
```
<link rel="alternate" hreflang="en" href="https://example.com/en/page">
<link rel="alternate" hreflang="es" href="https://example.com/es/page">
```

4. Example of Hreflang Tags for Country Targeting:
```
<link rel="alternate" hreflang="en-GB" href="https://example.com/uk/page">
<link rel="alternate" hreflang="en-US" href="https://example.com/us/page">
```

5. Implementing Hreflang Tags:
   - Place the hreflang tags in the head section of each page that has equivalent versions in different languages or regions.
   - Use self-referencing hreflang tags (e.g., `<link rel="alternate" hreflang="x-default" href="https://example.com/default/page">`) for the default language version of the page.

6. International URLs:
   - International URLs are specific URLs that target different languages or countries on your website.
   - Use separate URLs for each language or country version to differentiate the content.

7. URL Structure for Language Targeting:

- Use language subdirectories (e.g., example.com/en/ for English, example.com/es/ for Spanish).
- Use language subdomains (e.g., en.example.com, es.example.com).

8. URL Structure for Country Targeting:
  - Use country-code top-level domains (ccTLDs) (e.g., example.com.uk, example.com.au).
  - Use country subdirectories (e.g., example.com/uk/ for the United Kingdom, example.com/us/ for the United States).

9. Canonical URLs:
  - Implement canonical tags to indicate the preferred version of a page, especially for pages with similar content in different languages or regions.

10. Test and Monitor:
  - Test the implementation of hreflang tags and international URLs to ensure they are correctly set up.
  - Monitor webmaster tools and analytics to check for any errors or issues related to international targeting.

Properly implementing hreflang tags and international URLs is crucial for international SEO success. By doing so, you can improve the visibility of your website's content in specific languages and regions, deliver a more personalized user experience, and attract a broader international audience.

11.4 Content Localization and Translation
Content localization and translation are essential steps in expanding your website's reach to international markets. Localizing your content involves adapting it to suit the cultural, linguistic, and regional preferences of your target audience. Translation, on the other hand, refers to converting content from one language to another. Here's how to effectively implement content localization and translation:

1. Conduct Market Research:
  - Understand the cultural nuances, preferences, and sensitivities of your target international markets.
  - Identify which content requires localization and translation based on market research.

2. Localize Content Elements:
  - Localize various content elements, such as product descriptions, landing pages, calls-to-action, and images.
  - Adapt content to cater to the local market's preferences, including units of measurement, date formats, and currency symbols.

3. Use Professional Translators:
  - Hire professional translators who are native speakers of the target language and have expertise in the subject matter.
  - Avoid using machine translation tools for critical content as they may lead to inaccuracies.

4. Maintain Consistent Brand Voice:
  - Ensure that your brand voice remains consistent across different language versions.
  - Maintain the tone and style that align with your brand identity while adapting content for local audiences.

5. Implement Hreflang Tags:
  - Use hreflang tags to indicate language and regional targeting for your content, as discussed in the previous response.

6. Localize Visual Content:
  - Adapt images and visual content to resonate with the local culture and preferences.
  - Use images that feature people and settings familiar to the target audience.

7. Create Region-Specific Landing Pages:
  - Develop region-specific landing pages that address the unique needs and interests of local customers.
  - Customize content to showcase products or services most relevant to each region.

8. Proofreading and Editing:
  - Thoroughly proofread and edit translated content to ensure accuracy, clarity, and proper grammar.
  - Review content with native speakers to catch any cultural nuances that might have been missed.

9. Multilingual SEO:
  - Conduct keyword research for each target language and optimize content for relevant keywords.
  - Use localized keywords in meta titles, descriptions, and headings.

10. User-Generated Content:
   - Encourage user-generated content from customers in different languages and regions.
   - User reviews and testimonials in various languages can enhance credibility.

11. Monitor Performance:
   - Track the performance of localized content in each target market using web analytics tools.
   - Measure user engagement, conversions, and other relevant metrics to assess the effectiveness of your localization efforts.

Content localization and translation are crucial for connecting with international audiences on a deeper level. By delivering content tailored to their preferences and language, you can build trust and credibility, which, in turn, will drive engagement and conversions in the global market.

11.5 International Link Building Strategies
International link building strategies are essential for improving the authority and visibility of your website in international search results. Quality backlinks from reputable websites in different countries can enhance your global SEO efforts and help you connect with a broader international audience. Here are some effective international link building strategies:

1. Localized Content Marketing:
  - Create high-quality, relevant, and localized content for your target international markets.
  - Reach out to local influencers, bloggers, and industry websites to promote and link to your content.

2. Partner with Local Businesses:
  - Establish partnerships with relevant businesses in your target countries.
  - Collaborate on content, events, or promotions, and exchange backlinks to cross-promote each other's websites.

3. Local Directories and Citations:
   - Submit your website to local business directories and citation sites in your target countries.
   - Ensure that your business information is consistent across all directories.

4. Guest Blogging and Contributed Content:
   - Write guest blog posts for reputable websites in your target countries.
   - Offer valuable and informative content that showcases your expertise and includes relevant backlinks.

5. Translated Content Promotion:
   - If you have localized content in multiple languages, promote the translated versions to relevant websites in each language's region.
   - Seek backlinks from websites that cater to the language-speaking audience.

6. International PR and Outreach:
   - Conduct international PR and outreach campaigns to gain media coverage and mentions from international publications.
   - Press mentions and coverage can lead to valuable backlinks.

7. Participate in Global Events and Conferences:
   - Attend industry events and conferences in your target countries.
   - Network with other businesses and professionals to establish connections that may result in backlinks.

8. Social Media Outreach:
   - Engage with influential social media accounts and industry leaders in your target countries.
   - Build relationships and promote your content, which may lead to shares and backlinks.

9. Broken Link Building:
   - Identify broken links on relevant international websites in your niche.
   - Reach out to the site owners, notifying them of the broken link and suggesting your content as a replacement.

10. Create Link-Worthy Resources:
   - Develop link-worthy resources, such as comprehensive guides, infographics, or research reports.
   - Share these resources with websites that might find them valuable and willing to link back to them.

11. Monitor Competitor Backlinks:
   - Monitor the backlink profiles of your international competitors.
   - Identify potential link-building opportunities by approaching websites that link to your competitors.

12. Build Relationships with International Influencers:
   - Cultivate relationships with influential figures in your target countries.
   - Collaborate with them on content or promotions, which can lead to valuable backlinks.

Remember that international link building takes time and effort. Focus on creating valuable content and building genuine relationships with websites in your target countries. Gradually, your website's authority and visibility in the international market will improve, leading to increased organic traffic and broader global reach.

Chapter 12:
SEO Best Practices and Future Trends

12.1 Staying Ethical and Avoiding Black Hat SEO
Staying ethical and avoiding black hat SEO practices are essential for maintaining a sustainable and positive online presence. Black hat SEO techniques may provide short-term gains, but they can lead to severe penalties from search engines, damaging your website's reputation and long-term rankings. Here are some guidelines to ensure you practice ethical SEO and avoid black hat tactics:

1. Focus on Quality Content:
   - Create high-quality, valuable, and relevant content that meets the needs of your target audience.
   - Avoid keyword stuffing and provide genuine value through your content.

2. Follow Search Engine Guidelines:
   - Familiarize yourself with the guidelines and best practices provided by search engines like Google.
   - Adhere to these guidelines to ensure your website is in compliance with ethical SEO practices.

3. Avoid Keyword Stuffing:
   - Use keywords naturally and sparingly within your content.
   - Focus on user experience rather than excessively targeting keywords.

4. Build Natural Backlinks:
   - Earn backlinks from reputable and relevant websites through high-quality content and genuine relationships.
   - Avoid buying or exchanging links, as this violates search engine guidelines.

5. Say No to Cloaking and Hidden Text:
   - Do not use cloaking techniques to show different content to users and search engines.
   - Avoid hiding text or links to manipulate rankings.

6. Transparent Link Building:
   - Clearly disclose sponsored or affiliate links and ensure they do not pass PageRank (nofollow attribute).
   - Avoid using deceptive tactics to gain links.

7. Prioritize User Experience:
   - Design your website for the best user experience, including fast loading times, mobile-friendliness, and intuitive navigation.
   - Avoid disruptive pop-ups and intrusive ads.

8. Respect Copyright and Intellectual Property:
   - Use original images and content or properly attribute and obtain permission for copyrighted materials.
   - Avoid using content without permission or proper attribution.

9. No Automated or Low-Quality Content Generation:
   - Do not use automated content generation tools or spin content to create low-quality and duplicate content.
   - Focus on providing unique and valuable information.

10. Avoid Doorway Pages and Sneaky Redirects:
    - Do not create doorway pages designed solely for search engines with no value to users.
    - Avoid redirecting users to irrelevant pages.

11. Monitor Website Performance:
    - Regularly check for any unintentional technical issues or security breaches that may negatively impact your website.
    - Address any issues promptly.

12. Regularly Update and Improve:
    - Keep your website and content up-to-date and relevant.
    - Continuously improve user experience and stay informed about the latest SEO trends and best practices.

By adhering to ethical SEO practices, you build a strong and reputable online presence that stands the test of time. Organic growth through ethical means is a sustainable approach that enhances your website's credibility, user trust, and long-term search engine rankings.

12.2 Voice Search and SEO
Voice search is becoming increasingly popular as more people use voice-activated devices like smartphones, smart speakers, and virtual assistants to perform online searches. To optimize for voice search and improve your website's visibility in voice search results, consider the following SEO strategies:

1. Focus on Conversational Keywords:
   - Voice searches tend to be more conversational and natural than traditional typed queries.

- Optimize your content for long-tail and natural language keywords that people are likely to use when speaking.

2. Featured Snippets:
   - Featured snippets are concise answers displayed at the top of search results, often used for voice search responses.
   - Structure your content to provide clear and concise answers to commonly asked questions in your niche.

3. Local SEO for Voice:
   - Many voice searches are location-based (e.g., "near me" queries).
   - Optimize your website and Google My Business listing for local SEO to target voice searchers in your area.

4. Page Speed and Mobile-Friendliness:
   - Voice searches often come from mobile devices, so ensure your website is mobile-friendly and loads quickly.
   - Google prioritizes mobile-friendly sites in voice search results.

5. Use Structured Data:
   - Implement structured data markup (e.g., schema.org) to provide context and meaning to your content.
   - This helps search engines understand your content better and display relevant information in voice search results.

6. Natural Language Content:
   - Create content that sounds natural and conversational, addressing the needs and queries of your target audience.
   - Write in a way that matches how people talk, rather than using stiff or technical language.

7. FAQs and Q&A Pages:
   - Include an FAQ page on your website with common questions and answers related to your products or services.
   - Voice search often pulls answers directly from FAQ pages.

8. Local Business Information:
   - Ensure your website contains accurate and up-to-date information about your business, such as address, phone number, and business hours.
   - Voice searches often seek immediate answers, such as "What time does XYZ store open?"

9. Optimize for Featured Snippets:
   - Strive to provide concise answers to popular questions in your niche to increase your chances of appearing in featured snippets.

10. Monitor Voice Search Queries:
   - Use tools like Google Search Console and other analytics tools to monitor the voice search queries driving traffic to your site.
   - Analyze user behavior to identify opportunities for improvement.

11. Test Voice Search Queries:

- Experiment with voice search queries related to your business to see how your website appears in the results.
   - Understand how voice search impacts user intent and adjust your content accordingly.

12. Keep Up with Voice Search Trends:
   - Voice search technology is continually evolving, so stay updated with the latest trends and developments.
   - Adapt your SEO strategies accordingly to stay ahead in the voice search landscape.

By optimizing for voice search, you can position your website to capture valuable traffic from the growing number of users who prefer voice-activated search. By understanding and meeting the unique needs of voice searchers, you can enhance your overall SEO efforts and increase your website's visibility and engagement.

12.3 Mobile-First Indexing and SEO

Mobile-first indexing is a significant shift in how search engines like Google evaluate and rank websites. With mobile-first indexing, search engines primarily use the mobile version of a website's content to index and rank pages, even for searches conducted on desktop devices. To optimize your website for mobile-first indexing and improve your SEO performance, consider the following strategies:

1. Mobile-Friendly Design:
   - Ensure your website has a responsive design that adapts to different screen sizes and devices.
   - Use a mobile-friendly layout and design elements for optimal user experience on mobile devices.

2. Page Speed:
   - Improve your website's loading speed on mobile devices. Fast-loading pages provide a better user experience and positively impact SEO.
   - Use tools like Google PageSpeed Insights to identify and fix performance issues.

3. Mobile Usability:
   - Test your website's mobile usability with tools like Google's Mobile-Friendly Test.
   - Address any mobile usability issues, such as mobile-unfriendly fonts or elements that are too close together.

4. Avoid Flash:
   - Avoid using Adobe Flash, as it is not supported on many mobile devices and can negatively affect mobile SEO.

5. Accelerated Mobile Pages (AMP):
   - Consider implementing AMP to create lightweight and fast-loading versions of your pages, especially for content-heavy websites like blogs and news sites.

6. Optimize Images:
   - Compress images to reduce file sizes without compromising quality.
   - Use the appropriate image formats and implement lazy loading to improve mobile page loading times.

7. Clear and Concise Content:

- Present clear and concise content that is easy to read on mobile devices.
- Use shorter paragraphs, bullet points, and headings to break up text and make it scannable.

8. Mobile-Friendly Interstitials:
  - Avoid using intrusive pop-ups or interstitials that cover the main content on mobile devices.
  - Use mobile-friendly interstitials or banners that do not obstruct the user's view.

9. Mobile XML Sitemap:
  - Submit a separate XML sitemap for your mobile version to help search engines crawl and index your mobile content effectively.

10. Responsive Media:
  - Ensure videos, audio, and other media elements are responsive and compatible with various mobile devices.
  - Implement HTML5 for better mobile support.

11. Test on Mobile Devices:
  - Regularly test your website on various mobile devices and browsers to ensure a consistent and seamless user experience.

12. Mobile Site Audit:
  - Conduct a comprehensive mobile site audit to identify and fix any mobile-specific issues that may affect SEO and user experience.

By optimizing your website for mobile-first indexing, you enhance its performance in mobile search results, which is increasingly crucial as mobile usage continues to grow. Providing a positive mobile experience not only improves SEO rankings but also contributes to higher user engagement, longer visit durations, and increased conversions on mobile devices.

12.4 Artificial Intelligence and SEO
Artificial Intelligence (AI) is playing an increasingly significant role in the field of SEO, revolutionizing how search engines understand and rank web pages. AI-powered algorithms and tools are transforming the SEO landscape and presenting new opportunities for website owners to improve their search rankings and user experience. Here are some ways AI is influencing SEO:

1. Natural Language Processing (NLP):
  - AI-powered NLP enables search engines to better understand the context and intent behind search queries.
  - Websites can optimize content for more natural and conversational language, improving rankings for voice searches and long-tail keywords.

2. Rank Brain:
  - Rank Brain is an AI algorithm used by Google to help interpret complex search queries and deliver relevant search results.
  - Websites should focus on providing high-quality, relevant content to align with Rank Brain's preference for user-focused results.

3. Content Creation and Optimization:
  - AI tools can analyze search trends and user behavior to suggest content topics and optimization strategies.

- AI-generated content is becoming more advanced, but caution must be exercised to maintain authenticity and value.

4. Personalization:
   - AI algorithms can personalize search results based on user preferences, behavior, and location.
   - Websites should offer personalized content and recommendations to enhance user experience.

5. Image and Video Analysis:
   - AI can analyze and understand images and videos, providing context and information to search engines.
   - Optimizing images and videos with relevant metadata and descriptions helps search engines understand their content.

6. User Experience (UX) Optimization:
   - AI can analyze user behavior and engagement metrics to evaluate the quality of a website's user experience.
   - Websites should focus on providing a seamless, fast, and engaging user experience to improve rankings.

7. Predictive Analytics:
   - AI-powered predictive analytics can forecast changes in search behavior and market trends, enabling proactive SEO strategies.
   - Websites can use AI insights to optimize their content and stay ahead of competitors.

8. Technical SEO Automation:
   - AI can automate technical SEO tasks, such as crawling, indexing, and detecting website issues.
   - Websites benefit from improved technical SEO by ensuring smooth site performance and better crawlability.

9. Chatbots and Customer Support:
   - AI-powered chatbots provide instant customer support, improving user experience and engagement.
   - Websites can use chatbots to answer customer queries, enhance satisfaction, and improve SEO metrics.

10. Competitive Analysis:
   - AI tools can analyze competitors' SEO strategies and backlink profiles, identifying areas for improvement.
   - Websites can use AI insights to refine their own SEO tactics and stay competitive in their niche.

It's crucial for website owners to embrace AI-powered SEO tools and techniques to stay competitive and deliver a superior user experience. While AI offers numerous advantages, it's essential to maintain a balance between automation and human expertise to create valuable, user-centric content that aligns with search engine guidelines and best practices.

12.5 Future Trends and Adaptation in SEO

The field of SEO is continuously evolving, driven by advancements in technology, changes in user behavior, and updates to search engine algorithms. To stay ahead in the ever-changing landscape of

SEO, website owners and digital marketers must adapt to future trends. Here are some future trends and key areas of adaptation in SEO:

1. Voice Search Optimization:
   - Voice search is gaining popularity, and it's essential to optimize for voice-based queries.
   - Focus on long-tail, conversational keywords and featured snippets to capture voice search traffic.

2. Mobile-First Approach:
   - Mobile usage continues to grow, making a mobile-first approach crucial for SEO success.
   - Prioritize mobile responsiveness, page speed, and user experience on mobile devices.

3. AI and Machine Learning:
   - AI-powered algorithms are influencing search results and user experiences.
   - Embrace AI tools for content analysis, personalization, and predicting user behavior.

4. E-A-T and Content Quality:
   - Google's E-A-T (Expertise, Authoritativeness, Trustworthiness) algorithm emphasizes content quality and credibility.
   - Create authoritative and trustworthy content to improve rankings and user satisfaction.

5. Video and Visual Search:
   - Video content is increasingly popular, and visual search is on the rise.
   - Optimize videos with relevant metadata and transcripts for better visibility.
   - Use descriptive alt text for images to enhance visual search optimization.

6. Featured Snippets and Position Zero:
   - Featured snippets often appear at position zero in search results, capturing significant clicks.
   - Structure content to answer common questions directly, increasing the chances of being featured.

7. Local SEO and Google My Business:
   - Local SEO is vital for businesses with physical locations.
   - Optimize Google My Business profiles and focus on local citations for better local search visibility.

8. User Intent and Semantic Search:
   - Search engines are better understanding user intent through semantic search.
   - Optimize content to match user intent and provide comprehensive answers to queries.

9. Data Privacy and Security:
   - Website security and data privacy are becoming more critical for SEO rankings.
   - Implement HTTPS, protect user data, and follow privacy regulations to build trust with users.

10. Augmented Reality (AR) and Virtual Reality (VR):
    - AR and VR technologies are shaping the future of user experience.
    - Explore opportunities to leverage AR and VR in SEO strategies.

11. Customer Experience and Engagement:
    - User engagement metrics, such as click-through rates and dwell time, are increasingly important for SEO rankings.
    - Focus on providing valuable, engaging, and interactive content to keep users on your site.

12. Visual and Voice Search Advertising:
    - As visual and voice search grow, so does the potential for advertising in these formats.
    - Adapt your advertising strategies to include visual and voice search ads.

Incorporating these future trends into your SEO strategies will help you maintain a competitive edge and deliver valuable experiences to your audience. Stay informed about industry developments, track user behavior, and continuously analyze and optimize your SEO efforts to remain at the forefront of search engine rankings and user satisfaction.